Driving Successful Transformations

Defining Successful Transformation

Driving Successful Transformations

A Leader's Guide to Embracing and Executing Change

Jonathan Spiteri

BEP
BUSINESS EXPERT PRESS
Leader in applied, concise business books

Driving Successful Transformations:
A Leader's Guide to Embracing and Executing Change

First published in 2025 by
Business Expert Press, LLC
222 East 46th Street, New York, NY 10017
www.businessexpertpress.com

ISBN-13: 978-1-63742-925-9 (hardcover)
ISBN-13: 978-1-63742-902-0 (paperback)
ISBN-13: 978-1-63742-903-7 (e-book)

Human Resource Management and Organizational Behavior Collection

First edition: 2025

10 9 8 7 6 5 4 3 2 1

EU SAFETY REPRESENTATIVE
Mare Nostrum Group B.V.
Mauritskade 21D
1091 GC Amsterdam
The Netherlands
gpsr@mare-nostrum.co.uk

Dedication

To those who've shaped my path, both through encouragement and adversity, for teaching me the power of perseverance and the importance of never giving up on my dreams.

To my wife and children, the lights in my life, thank you for your love, patience, and endless belief in me. This book is as much yours as it is mine.

Description

Disruption is no longer an anomaly; it is the norm. From technological advancements to shifting consumer expectations, being able to transform and adapt to change is no longer a luxury that companies can afford to experiment with but rather a requisite for their existence and growth.

Studies show that the majority of change initiatives fail to deliver their intended outcomes. Why? Because transformation cannot be treated as a simple strategy or a project. Instead, it must be a journey that requires alignment, adaptability, and commitment at every level of an organization.

This book is rooted in the belief that a successful transformation is about more than tools and frameworks; it's about mindset, culture, and people. At its core, this book embodies the SHIFT philosophy, a framework that goes beyond a step-by-step process to offer an iterative, adaptable approach for navigating transformation. This framework - Start, Harmonize, Integrate, Facilitate, and Transform - is designed to address the human and cultural dynamics alongside other mechanics of transformation that often determine success or failure.

Whether launching a small-scale project or driving a companywide transformation as a C-level executive, senior manager, change manager, or change consultant, this book provides practical tools, actionable insights, and a holistic mindset to navigate challenges, align stakeholders, and actualize the organization's transformational vision.

With its simple, accessible style, this book is also a valuable resource for individuals seeking professional development and leadership skills, or academic researchers focusing on organizational studies, leadership, and innovation.

Contents

x CONTENTS

List of Figures

Testimonials

Driving Successful Transformations manages quite eloquently to break down the complexity of change management within an organizational environment to a doable set of iterative stages, that untangles and then reconfigures the organization and its resource base towards a new 'north star' vision. The SHIFT framework created by the author effectively combines top-down strategizing with bottom-up tactical actions, using practical implementation tips, detailed examples, and a powerful toolbox to guide the reader through every stage of the change process. Definitely a must read!

—Dr Ing Alex Rizzo B.ENG, MBA, DBA, FIET, FCIWEM

Driving Successful Transformations is a clear and practical guide for leaders ready to navigate real change. Jonathan's SHIFT model breaks down the journey into actionable stages - but what sets this book apart is its focus on people.

He reminds us that transformation is never just a process - it's a human journey rooted in mindset, culture, and trust. As he writes, *"A successful transformation is about more than tools and frameworks; it's about mindset, culture, and people."*

He treats communication as the engine of change, showing how trust and clear dialogue align people behind a shared vision. Instead of fighting resistance, he urges leaders to turn it into resilience - a perspective every executive coach will appreciate.

With its balance of strategy, practical tools, and real-world insights, this book is a timely reminder that sustainable transformation succeeds or fails with people at its heart.

Jonathan Spiteri's book blends strategy and humanity. If you're leading change - or about to - it will help you ask the right questions, engage your people, and keep your transformation on track. A thoughtful guide for any leader's shelf.

—Cathryn O'Donnelly, Careers Specialist & Organizational Coach

Preface

The only constant in the world of business is change. Companies that embrace change as a normal and expected facet of their existence, rather than as a threat, are those companies that ultimately thrive. The reality is that being able to transform and adapt to change is no longer a luxury that companies can afford to experiment with but rather a necessary requisite for their existence and growth.

Pushing for a company's transformation is not an easy task. It requires a fundamental shift in mindset, one that brings with it a willingness to challenge the status quo alongside a clear, achievable vision for the future. Businesses must have leaders who are able to inspire and motivate teams to take on change, even when it is uncomfortable or uncertain. Customers and their evolving needs must be deeply understood, while technology and data must be properly leveraged to drive innovation and efficiency. All of these make transformations complex, challenging, and hard to execute.

Writing this book has been a product of years of personal experience working with many organizations that spanned various industries and countries, guiding each with their own transformative journeys. These experiences have given me the opportunity to witness firsthand the challenges, setbacks, and triumphs faced by these changing companies. The power of a clear vision, the importance of a workforce's adaptability, and the potential of technology and innovation have consistently stood out as core tenets of successful company transformations.

Each of my experiences with change in companies, whether positive or negative, has helped contribute toward a holistic understanding of what is behind successful transformations. The insights and perspectives espoused in this book have been shaped by my observations of inspiring leaders who demonstrated commitment to their vision, teams with remarkable resilience who overcame adversities, and challenging moments that tested my own resolve.

Writing this book has been both a challenging and rewarding experience, during which I have distilled multifaceted and complex concepts into strategies and actionable insights. This has led me to define a comprehensive framework that helps organizations guide their transformation efforts effectively. The objective of this framework is not only to outline the necessary steps for a successful change but to consistently remind and encourage organizations to consider the complexities behind human behavior, organizational culture, and their dynamics. All in the hopes of finding the right balance between innovation and execution throughout their transformation journey.

I have called the resulting guide the "SHIFT framework." This model breaks down transformations into distinct, but interconnected stages, considering elements such as understanding the need for change, aligning organizational efforts, integrating key elements and facilitating innovation. However, the focus should always remain on how to ensure sustainable success throughout the whole journey.

This book aims to equip CEOs, senior managers, and change management professionals with the knowledge, tools and strategies for a successful transformation. Change is challenging, but with the right guidance and openness to learning, it can also be one of the most rewarding journeys your organization will ever undertake.

A transformative journey lies ahead. Let's embark on it together.

Jonathan Spiteri

Ancillary Resources

Ancillary materials accompany the book to support both individual study and classroom learning. These include dedicated questions for the case study featured at the end of each stage of the SHIFT Framework, accessible via the QR code below, as well as additional supporting resources available on request via marketing@businessexpertpress.com.

Together, these materials are designed to help readers apply the framework in practice, reinforce key ideas, and provide instructors with tools to reference the book and encourage classroom discussion.

You can access the case study questions here:

Acknowledgments

I would like to give my sincere thanks to Sean Montebello for his careful eye, editorial feedback, and commitment to the manuscript's refinement. My deep gratitude also extends to Luke Agius, whose illustrations and visual aids are invaluable to succinctly communicate this book's core messages and breathe life into this work.

Introducing the SHIFT Framework

The Urgency of Adaptation

Picture this: A company, once a leader within its field, is now struggling to stay afloat. Its customers are turning to competitors that are newer and have a faster response to market demands. Its employees feel disengaged and demoralized. Its once-innovative products are now seen as outdated and irrelevant.

This isn't a hypothetical scenario; it's a reality that businesses in different industries have to repeatedly face.

Many such organizations resist the inevitable need for change. They cling to outdated practices and avoid stepping outside their comfort zones. What is not immediately apparent is that the cost of such inaction is high.

Such stagnation breeds complacency, in turn breeding irrelevance.

The data paints a stark picture:

- Between 70 percent and 90 percent of large-scale change programs fail to achieve their stated goals.[1]
- Digitally immature companies are 26 percent less profitable than their industry competitors, according to an *MIT Sloan Management Review* study.[2]
- Only 4 in 10 employees are aware of what their organization is trying to achieve.[3]

---

[1]M. Higgs and D. Rowland, "All Changes Great and Small: Exploring Approaches to Change and Its Leadership," *Journal of Change Management* 11, no. 2 (2011): 121-151.

[2]G. Westerman, D. Bonnet, and A. McAfee, *Leading Digital: Turning Technology into Business Transformation* (Harvard Business Press, 2014).

[3]Forbes Business Council, "The Case for Transparency in the Workplace and Its Impact on Organizational Performance," *Forbes*, June 16, 2023, https://www.forbes.com/councils/forbesbusinesscouncil/2023/06/16/the-case-for-transparency-in-the-workplace-and-its-impact-on-organizational-performance/.

These numbers highlight just how challenging it is for an organization to undertake a transformation. At the same time, transformations present a tremendous opportunity for those who recognize change as a catalyst for growth. This book will guide you through a structured and actionable framework - the SHIFT model - to transform your organization from the inside out.

The SHIFT framework will empower you with the knowledge, tools, and strategies to lead your organization successfully through a transformation, setting the stage for a future where you not only survive but become the leader in your industry.

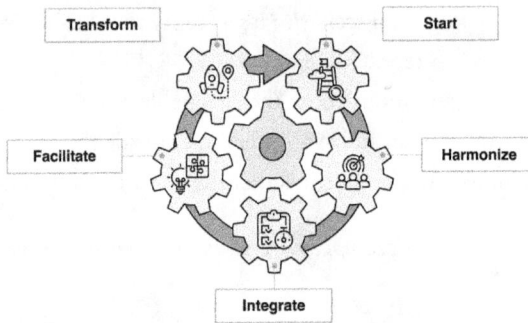

Figure 1: The SHIFT framework

The SHIFT Framework: Your Roadmap to Transformation

Stage 1: Start (S)

Every journey begins with a single step. Recognizing the need for change is the first step to transforming your organization - a foundational stage within the SHIFT framework.

This stage involves more than just acknowledging the necessity for change; it's about establishing an understanding of the need for transformation, assessing organizational readiness, and defining a compelling vision that will guide your efforts going forward.

This stage is tackled across the next three key chapters, each building upon the last to ensure a solid foundation for your organization's transformation:

- *Chapter 1: Understanding the Need for Transformation*
  Does your organization elicit a nagging sense of stagnation? Are your competitors outpacing you? Are your customers voicing dissatisfaction? This chapter will help you identify signals for the need of an organizational change, along with the drivers (both internal and external) pushing you toward transformation.

- *Chapter 2: Organizational Readiness Assessment*
  Before setting off on your change journey, it's essential to understand whether you're equipped for the trip. This chapter will help you evaluate how ready your organization is for change. Its structure, processes, and workflows will be examined, along with the current technological infrastructure and the abilities of your employees. This thorough assessment will show strengths and weaknesses, allowing you to tailor your strategy accordingly.

- *Chapter 3: Defining Your Transformation Vision*
  Once you understand both why change is needed and your organization's current capabilities, you must set your sights on the path ahead. This chapter will outline how a clear, compelling, and customer-centric vision for change can be crafted. This "North Star" will inspire and guide your organization through every step of the transformation journey.

By the end of stage 1, you'll have a deep understanding of why your organization needs to transform, a comprehensive assessment of its readiness for change, and a "North Star" vision of what you would like to achieve. This foundation is essential for the successful implementation of the SHIFT framework's remaining stages, ensuring that your effective transformation is also sustainable in the long term.

Stage 2: Harmonize (H)

Once you have laid out the groundwork, as the conductor of this transformation, you must orchestrate harmony within your organization. This entails aligning every element of your organization, whether strategic plans, company culture, or leadership actions for a unified approach to change.

The end goal of this stage is to foster a collaborative environment where each staff member is moving in unison, actively invested in achieving the "North Star" vision you have previously established. Aside from developing a detailed plan, this stage demands a fundamental shift in mindset, a willingness to embrace change, and a leadership style that embodies these values.

In this section, we dissect the "Harmonize" step into three pillars:

- *Chapter 4: Planning for Transformation Success*
  This chapter lays the groundwork for harmony by providing a roadmap for change. It helps leaders analyze gaps, prioritize initiatives, and align resources, paving the way for a clear and focused path forward. This alignment prevents confusion and ensures that everyone is working toward the same goals.

- *Chapter 5: Building a Culture of Change*
  This chapter focuses on the "hearts and minds" behind the transformation. By fostering a growth mindset, encouraging continuous learning, and establishing the normality of change, you create an environment where employees do not just accept change but actively embrace it. This cultural alignment is essential for overcoming resistance and sustaining your transformation's momentum.

- *Chapter 6: Leading The Change*
  This chapter emphasizes the importance of strong leadership for change. It explores the specific qualities and behaviors that leaders must embody to inspire, motivate, and guide their teams through their organization's transformation.

Thorough investment in the "Harmonize" stage means not just preparing your team for change but paving the way for a unified transformation journey. You'll equip your workforce with the mindset and skills to embrace new challenges and actively contribute to your organization's "North Star" vision. This foundation of harmony and empowerment will fuel the next phases of your journey, where innovation and action take center stage.

Stage 3: Integrate (I)

You have so far defined your vision, prepared your leaders, and built a change-ready culture within your organization. Now it's time to make these elements a cohesive whole, integrating them into the core of your organization.

To achieve your "North Star," it is essential to ensure that communication, adaptability, and resistance management are integrated well together in such a way that they strategically reinforce each other. This empowers your workforce and paves the way for sustainable transformation.

The Integrate stage encompasses three key aspects:

- *Chapter 7: Communication as the Engine of Change*
  Communicating effectively is not just about relaying information. The skill involves building trust, inspiring action within your employees, and creating a unified understanding of your vision for the transformation. It involves listening actively to feedback, tailoring your messages to your respective audience and establishing an ongoing dialogue within your organization.

- *Chapter 8: Fostering an Adaptable Workforce*
  For a successful transformation, your workforce must be pre-equipped to embrace it and adapt to the unforeseen challenges it may bring. This chapter tackles the strategies behind fostering a learning-oriented work culture, finding and addressing gaps in skills and empowering your workforce into an active participant in the change.

- *Chapter 9: Turning Resistance Into Resilience*
  Resistance is a normal and expected part of change, but if it isn't effectively addressed, it can derail your transformation. This chapter looks at the root causes of resistance, delineates strategies for overcoming it, and highlights the importance of turning resistance into adaptive and thriving resilience.

By the end of the "Integration" stage, you will have successfully built a culture that embraces change. At one end, your employees, now equipped with a growth mindset and engaged in continuous learning, are ready to contribute to your transformative vision. At the other end, your leaders, able to communicate effectively and swiftly addressing resistance, are ready to guide the organization through the complexities of change. By making these two ends meet, you will have created an environment where innovation is encouraged, setting the stage for your organization to evolve and thrive in the face of any disruption.

Stage 4: Facilitate (F)

Once a change-ready culture and effective communication have been established, it's time to move from general readiness into the specific actions that enable innovation.

In this stage, we'll focus on building the structures, processes, and systems that will allow your team to turn their creative ideas into tangible outcomes. Your transformation gains momentum through this facilitation, fueled by a continuous cycle of experimentation and learning. This stage bridges the "what" (your vision) to the "how" (the practical actions needed to achieve it).

This stage is explored through three chapters:

- *Chapter 10: Innovation as a Core Driver*
  Beyond buzzwords, this chapter shows why innovation is essential for transformations. An innovative organization does more than just product development, instead it takes advantage of opportunities for improvement in every aspect of your business. We'll delve into different types of innovation -from incremental tweaks

to radical disruptions in established processes - and discuss how to strategically choose the right approach for your needs.

- *Chapter 11: Fostering an Innovation Ecosystem*
  This chapter is your blueprint for turning your organization into an innovation "machine." You'll discover how to foster safe spaces that allow for experimentation, moving away from the misconception that failures are setbacks for your transformation. Instead, they should be considered a golden source for learning opportunities that will help you steer your actions and smoothen your transformation journey. Finally we'll discuss the need for defining leadership strategies that will set the correct tone for your transformation, restructuring teams and your organization to allow agility, investing in the right resources to boost innovation, and using data to fuel your innovation engine.

- *Chapter 12: Experimentation and Learning Loops*
  This is where your innovation truly takes flight. We'll explore the art and science of experimentation, showing you how to design experiments that maximize effectiveness, rapidly prototype new ideas, and leverage data to refine your approach. This chapter looks at how continuous learning and improvement loops are built, ensuring that transformation efforts remain agile and responsive, while constantly evolving to meet the needs of your customers and your market.

By the end of stage 4, you will have built a thriving ecosystem for innovation within your organization. This involves safe spaces for experimentation, empowered teams that generate and willingly share ideas, and successfully aligned resources that reward and support cyclical and continuous learning and improvement.

Stage 5: Transform (T)

By this stage your transformation no longer remains a vision or a plan; it's a journey in motion, with all its twists and turns, challenges and triumphs. This stage is about the active implementation and management of change. It ensures that your strategic initiatives deliver the desired results, effectively steering your organization toward its "North Star" while remaining adaptable to the ever-changing landscape.

To guide you through this exciting final phase, we'll delve into these key chapters:

- *Chapter 13: Choosing the Right Change Management Frameworks*
  This chapter explores the various change management frameworks available, from classic models like Kotter's Eight-Step Process to agile approaches. You'll learn how to choose the framework that best suits your organization's unique needs and culture, laying the groundwork for a smooth and effective transformation.

- *Chapter 14: Technology and Data as Transformation Enablers*
  This chapter explores how technology and data can drive and support change. We'll delve into how critical it is to use technology as an accelerant for change and how empowering your team with the right tools and insights will lead to success. We'll also discuss how to ensure data quality, governance, and security, so you can make informed decisions throughout the whole journey.

- *Chapter 15: Keeping on Track*
  Transformation is not a linear process; it's a meandering journey of learning and adaptation. This chapter looks at the tools and strategies that help track your progress, identify and mitigate risks, and make necessary adjustments to ensure your transformation remains aligned with your "North Star" and delivers lasting results.

By the end of this stage, you will have selected and tailored the ideal change management framework for your organization, understood how technology and data can support you during your transformation journey, and established a robust system for monitoring progress and mitigating risks. With these tools and knowledge, you'll lead your team confidently through the transformation journey, ensuring that your efforts are not only effective but also aligned with your overall vision and goals.

How the SHIFT Framework Works

The SHIFT framework is designed to guide your organization through successful transformation by dividing and addressing every critical aspect of change. It is a dynamic and iterative process that ensures flexibility and adaptability. Each stage builds upon the previous, creating a continuous cycle of assessment, alignment, integration, facilitation, and transformation. Here's how the SHIFT framework works as a whole.

Dynamic and Iterative Process

Flexibility and Adaptability

The SHIFT framework is not a linear, one-time process. It's designed to be dynamic and iterative, meaning that you can move back and forth between stages as needed. This flexibility allows for crucial responses to unexpected challenges and opportunities that will arise during the transformation journey, offering a distinct advantage over frameworks and models that require strict adherence.

Continuous Improvement

As you progress through each stage, you gather insights and learnings that inform the subsequent stages. This cycle of continuous improvement ensures that your transformation strategy remains relevant and effective, adapting to changes both within and outside your organization.

Stage-by-Stage Integration

The SHIFT framework's strength lies in how each stage seamlessly integrates with the others, creating a cohesive and comprehensive approach to transformations. Starting by establishing a clear understanding of the need for change and assessing organizational readiness, these insights consequently drive the alignment of organizational culture, leadership, and planning efforts in the "Harmonize" stage.

Once these elements are aligned, the focus shifts to integrating key components such as effective communication, adaptability, and resistance management into the very core of your organization. This integration en-sures that the groundwork laid in the previous stages supports a resilient and adaptable workforce, capable of embracing and driving change.

Facilitating a supportive innovation ecosystem builds on this inte-grated foundation, building an environment where innovation and con-tinuous improvement become a norm. The iterative nature of the SHIFT framework means that the ideas and feedback generated in this stage can loop back to refine and enhance the alignment and integration stages, creating cyclical growth and adaptability.

Finally, the Transform stage leverages all the previous work by ensur-ing your transformation remains on course using appropriate frameworks and methodologies, project management techniques, and technology. This stage draws on the integrated efforts of the previous stages, monitor-ing progress and making necessary adjustments, ultimately ensuring that the transformation remains on track and aligned with the strategic vision.

Creating a Continuous Cycle

Feedback Loops

At each stage, feedback loops are established to ensure ongoing assess-ment and realignment as necessary. For example, during the Transform stage, regular reviews and adjustments may loop back to the Integrate stage to address any emerging resistance or gaps in communication.

Learning and Adaptation

The iterative nature of the SHIFT framework means that learning and adaptation are constant. Each cycle through the stages allows the organi-zation to refine its approach, ensuring that the transformation is always moving in the right direction.

Strategic Alignment and Execution

Throughout the SHIFT framework, the North Star vision established in the Start stage serves as the whole transformation's guiding light. All activities, from cultural alignment to innovation, are strategically aligned with this vision to ensure cohesive and focused transformation efforts. Various methodologies and tools, such as change management frameworks, project management techniques, and data analytics, are used to ensure that each stage is executed with precision and effectiveness.

Your Transformation Starts Now

The SHIFT framework is designed to guide you through the complex and often challenging process of organizational transformation. It provides a structured, yet flexible approach that can be tailored to your specific needs and goals.

This overview has given you a glimpse of the path ahead, highlighting the five key stages of Start, Harmonize, Integrate, Facilitate, and Transform. Each stage builds upon the insights of previous stages, creating a continuous cycle of assessment, alignment, action, and adaptation.

The true power of transformation, however, lies in its practical application. In the upcoming chapters, we'll delve deep into each stage, looking at the practical tools, strategies, and real-world examples you need to turn your vision into reality.

Whether you're facing a minor shift or a radical overhaul, the time to transform is now.

Are you ready to take the leap?

STAGE 1

Start

CHAPTER 1

Understanding the Need for Transformation

"If you know the enemy and know yourself, you need not fear the result of a hundred battles."

—Sun Tzu, *The Art of War*

Introduction: The Crossroads of Change

> **?** Have you ever driven past a familiar landmark only to realize it's been altered, remodeled, or demolished?

Change is inevitable, and organizations are not exempt from it. It's useless to question whether your organization will face change - the harsh reality is that it will, either through external or internal pressures. The determiner for success is whether it will be a transformation you lead or one you are forced to react to.

While the idea of leading change can be inspiring for many, the reality of embarking on an organizational transformation is undeniably challenging. It involves dealing with resistance to your ideas, financial and logistical considerations, and numerous other obstacles.

Yet, postponing change carries an even greater risk - one that potentially threatens your organization's very existence.

This makes it imperative to recognize the signals for the necessity of change before you find yourself in a crisis. As in all aspects of life, reacting under pressure increases the likelihood of costly mistakes due to rushed decisions. The only way to avoid this challenge is by proactively staying vigilant and embracing continual transformation, positioning your organization for success.

Think about the future - with this mindset of proactive information gathering, ask yourself:

> **?** If no changes are made, where will your organization be five years from now? Will it be a stagnant relic, desperately clinging to outdated models? Or will it stand as a leader in the industry, renowned for its adaptability and exceptional ability to exceed customer expectations?

The path you choose today will determine that future.

Identifying Signs of Stagnation

Stagnation is a threat to organizations. Despite this, it's a threat you can overcome by closely monitoring specific factors that highlight where your organization might be losing ground. Eventually, this knowledge will enable you to take decisive action that addresses the challenges that are keeping you stagnant.

Diminishing Market Share

A shrinking market share is a clear warning sign that organizations cannot afford to ignore. Data shows that companies experiencing this decline are significantly more likely to fail within a few years.

However, recognizing the problem isn't enough.

To ensure your response is effective, you need to pinpoint the root reasons behind that decline. Ask yourself critical questions such as:

> **?** Is your organization losing ground due to better competitor offerings, evolving customer preferences, or an inability to innovate?

Remember, genuine answers for these questions are crucial. As a result, you need strong leaders who prioritize acknowledging facts and finding solutions over shifting blame and skirting responsibility.

Ultimately, identifying the root cause, or causes, of market share loss is the first step toward understanding which areas of your business require transformation to secure your organization's future success.

Customer Dissatisfaction

Think of customer satisfaction as the pulse of your organization. When it weakens, the very survival of your business is at risk. Whether it's declining product quality, outdated service models, or simply not meeting customer needs, dissatisfaction is a red flag demanding immediate attention.

For example, an online retailer facing frequent returns due to inaccurate product descriptions needs to urgently revamp, not only its listings but potentially its entire approach to quality control. Failure to address this would mean a misalignment between what you are offering and what your customers truly want and need.

Just as you prioritize regular health checkups, make sure that you proactively monitor customer satisfaction by investing in the right tools and working to build an organizational culture that views every sign of dissatisfaction as an urgent call to action and an opportunity for improvement.

Time-to-Market

> **?** Can your competitors consistently bring new products or services to market faster than you?

If so, this is a strong sign that the way your organization innovates needs to change.

Besides immediate suspects such as outdated technology or inefficient processes, an innovation-stifling culture is often the real culprit behind such issues. Such a culture exists if your organization fears change, lacks a focused strategy for innovation, or is paralyzed by bureaucracy.

Imagine a company where every new idea faces endless approval layers, where failure is punished, and risk-taking is discouraged. Do those conditions allow for quick innovation?

Instead, processes must be proactively streamlined, employees should be empowered to contribute ideas, and a culture of calculated risk-taking and continuous improvement should be encouraged and rewarded. Apart from improving your time-to-market, bringing down these internal innovation barriers will position your organization for sustainable and long-term success.

Evolving Competitive Landscape

Organizations often underestimate the quick pace of change in the contemporary competitive landscape. While the status quo may appear stable, new entrants constantly emerge trying to carve out their own piece of the market share.

> **?** Are you surprised when disruptive start-ups enter your industry or when established rivals suddenly offer something radically different?

Many organizations, especially larger and longer-established ones, lack the mechanisms, and sometimes even the motivation, to proactively monitor their industry. This can lead to blindness not just toward immediate rivals, but broader trends and potential disruptors who could reshape their entire landscape. This failure to anticipate change has dire consequences, hindering an organization's ability to protect itself, take advantage of opportunities, and solidify its competitive advantage.

Regulatory and Compliance Pressures

Industries that are highly regulated necessitate an organization's ability to rapidly adapt to new rules and requirements. As a result, you should be asking yourself:

> **?** Are you consistently finding it difficult to keep up with regulatory changes, consequently resorting to quick fixes and reactive solutions?

Obsolescent technology, inefficiencies in processes, and a "bare minimum" compliance culture will inevitably lead to costly oversights and put your organization at risk. Instead, regulatory change implementations should be seen as opportunities to improve your processes and upgrade technology.

Keep in mind that by staying ahead of regulatory changes, you will not only avoid penalties but you could also gain efficiencies. This could potentially gain you a competitive advantage over those who struggle to comply with these changes.

Employee Disengagement and High Turnover

Chronic employee disengagement and high turnover rates are more than just problems for the HR department - they are flashing warning signs that signal deeper issues within your organization that threaten its long-term success. Low employee engagement and poor morale stifle innovation, hinder project delivery, and ultimately, damage customer relations. Furthermore, when talented employees leave frequently, your organization loses its most valuable asset - the knowledge and experience that these employees would have accumulated over the years.

Faced with this situation, you should consider undergoing transformations aimed at changing your organizational culture to one that values employees, offers opportunities for growth, and helps staff understand how their work contributes to the organization's goals. Such transformations usually require you to invest in leadership development in order to create a sense of open communication, purpose, and belonging within the organization.

Case
Study

Case Study: Kodak Versus Netflix
Company Name: Kodak

Overview:

At its peak, Kodak held a huge share of its market and had excellent brand loyalty. However, its failure to move from film to digital photography led to its eventual bankruptcy in 2012.

Change Approach:

- *Fear of Cannibalizing Existing Business*: Ironically, Kodak was one of the first companies to invent digital camera technology. However, it depended on a revenue model built on film and photo processing. Fearing that digital would cannibalize their highly profitable film business, Kodak resisted investing in the new technology.

- *Focus on Incremental, Not Disruptive Innovation*: Kodak eventually did slowly shift toward digital. Unfortunately, its approach was focused on protecting its traditional business. They released hybrid products in an attempt to ease customers into the digital era, instead of boldly embracing the technology's potential disruption.

- *Risk-Averse Culture*: Kodak stifled its own innovations by fearing risks. This prevented the company from decisively pivoting toward digital when gaining a substantial market foothold was still possible.

- *Missed Opportunities in the Digital Age*: By keeping their focus on film and printed photography, Kodak missed out on opportunities to enter digital photo sharing and camera phone markets.

- *Failure to Adapt to Changing Customer Preferences*: Despite clear evidence that customers were embracing the convenience of digital photography, Kodak clung to a model that was becoming inconvenient and slow relative to the emerging digital alternatives.

Result:

Kodak managed to emerge from bankruptcy as a smaller, niche company. While they survived, their fall from market leader illustrates the importance of:

- Embracing disruptive technologies rather than fearing them.

- Understanding and adapting to shifting customer needs and behaviors.
- Fostering a culture that encourages risk-taking and forward-thinking.

Company Name: Netflix

Overview:

Originally a DVD mail-rental service, Netflix's true success lies in their pivot to video streaming. They adapted their business model, anticipating and embracing changes in the market, technology, and user preferences.

Change Approach:

- *Early Embrace of Streaming*: While competitors like Blockbuster didn't change their brick-and-mortar model, Netflix recognized the potential of video streaming and invested heavily in this technology while it was still in its early stages.

- *Customer-Centric Focus*: Netflix made use of user data to understand viewing habits, preferences, and pain points. Their recommendation algorithms and the seamless user experience on their streaming platforms became key differentiators.

- *Content as a Competitive Advantage*: Netflix evolved beyond solely offering licensed content. They invested heavily in producing original content, giving users a unique reason to subscribe and stay engaged with their platform.

- *Focus on Agility*: Netflix took the plunge and discarded elements of their business that were no longer serving their growth. They shut down the DVD by mail service to focus entirely on streaming. This adaptability allowed them to stay ahead of the curve.

- *Global Vision*: Unlike many U.S.-centric media giants, Netflix recognized the massive potential in international markets, and through the use of technology tailored their platform and content offerings accordingly.

Result:

Netflix disrupted the traditional entertainment industry, moving from a mail-rental service to a global streaming powerhouse with productions in numerous countries and languages. Their ability to repeatedly transform showcases the power of:

- Visionary leadership willing to adapt the core business model.
- Leveraging technology for customer convenience and new markets.
- Relentless focus on the evolving needs of the consumer.

The signs of stagnation should not be taken lightly. Ignoring these critical signs invites decline, making future transformations more difficult while potentially jeopardizing your organization's long-term prospects.

As these two case studies have shown us, no company, regardless of its past success, is immune to the need for transformation. Where Kodak was held back by its fear of cannibalizing its existing business and status quo, Netflix boldly reimagined itself multiple times over. These cases demonstrate that agility and the willingness to evolve are crucial for any organization's survival and long-term success in the contemporary landscape.

External Versus Internal Drivers of Change

The stagnation signs we've discussed rarely appear overnight. Often, they're the result of forces that have been at play for some time, both outside and within your organization. For this reason, it is crucial to understand these change drivers as they will help you define a vision for your transformation, set the right targets, and align key stakeholders behind your initiatives.

Here's a closer look at these change drivers:

External Drivers

Externally driven change is that which is prompted through factors outside your organization. While forces within the larger, external business market can be disruptive, they present significant opportunities if proactively identified and adapted to.

Some of these external drivers include:

- *Technological Advancements*
  Emergent and innovative changes in technology are continuously disruptive through their offer of previously unavailable possibilities. If an organization refuses to embrace these opportunities, such as refusing the adoption of automation or artificial intelligence (AI), it risks becoming obsolete. Think Netflix's disruptions of the traditional video rental industry with its streaming model, rendering companies like Blockbuster irrelevant.

- *Economic Shifts*
  Understanding the current economic situation is crucial when determining the focus of your transformation. In difficult times, the transformation might center on efficiency and finding new revenue streams, while in periods of growth, investing in innovation may take center stage.

- *Shifts in Customer Behavior*
  Cultural shifts, societal trends, and global events continuously change customers' and clients' behaviors and needs, creating pressure on organizations to adapt. Understanding these needs before taking on a transformation is vital for success. For instance, increasing demand for ethically sourced products is pushing companies to rethink their entire supply chains.

- *Market Dynamics and Competition*
  Competitors within your field come and go constantly. Monitoring for new entrants, changing customer preferences, and global market shifts helps organizations understand where they must adapt to remain relevant and competitive. For example, are new players with subscription-based models disrupting your industry? Have long-time rivals expanded into adjacent markets?

  Proactively analyzing these shifts is essential to protecting your market share.

- *Regulatory Changes*
  New laws and regulations, especially in highly regulated fields, are a major driver of change. Proactive organizations view compliance with these policy changes as an opportunity to innovate, improve processes, and gain a competitive advantage. Consider the impact of the General Data Protection Regulation (GDPR) on data privacy - organizations that embraced this shift positioned themselves as leaders in protecting consumer information.

Internal Drivers

Understanding the external landscape is crucial, but let's turn our attention inward. Organizations also face internal pressures that trigger the need for transformation, some of which include:

- *Outdated Processes*
  Inefficient or cumbersome processes hinder agility. These lead to a longer time to market, and potentially reduce your ability to innovate in products and services. Process reengineering requires careful management of stakeholders and strategic planning to avoid rushed, ineffective changes.

- *Obsolete Technology Infrastructure*
  Legacy systems and outdated technology create barriers to growth and innovation. Attempts to address this with quick-fix solutions that don't integrate with existing systems often lead to higher long-term costs and additional performance issues. This drives technology-focused transformations that streamline your technology stack and can even reimagine core processes.

- *Employees*
  Employees themselves can be a catalyst for change. High turnover or difficulty introducing new ideas might signal the need for a culture shift toward adaptability, innovation, and overcoming barriers to change.

Furthermore, your workforce must be able to evolve with the changing environment. Proactively identifying where current skills fall short and having a plan to upskill or attract new talent is crucial.

- *Lack of Collaboration*
  Departmental silos are a common problem in large organizations as this creates redundancies, duplications of effort, and hampers the cross-functional collaboration often essential for innovative problem-solving.

Keep in mind that the goal of understanding these internal drivers of change is not to assign blame but rather to comprehend what is limiting your organization's ability to achieve certain goals. Understanding both internal and external forces for change will allow you to develop truly effective transformation strategies. This knowledge will help you address the root causes of the issues you're facing, ultimately positioning your organization for resilience, innovation, and the ability to thrive among the constantly evolving landscape.

Key Takeaways

- *Change Is Inevitable:* Stagnation is a warning sign, not a permanent state. Proactive organizations recognize that transformation is essential for continued success.
- *External and Internal Drivers: Understanding both types of forces influencing your organization* is crucial for developing effective transformation strategies.
- *Action-Oriented Focus:* It's not enough to just recognize the need for change. Identifying concrete areas for improvement (processes, technology, culture) empowers you to act.
- *Transformation as Opportunity:* While change can be daunting, view it as a chance to build resilience, become more innovative, and strengthen your competitive position.

CHAPTER 2

Organizational Readiness Assessment

"The secret of getting ahead is getting started."

—Mark Twain

Introduction: Are You Ready for the Journey?

Imagine going on a cross-country road trip while contending with these conditions:

1. You have no map.
2. Your car needs maintenance.
3. Half of your passengers are unsure they even want to go on this journey.

The odds of success are obviously quite slim ….

The same applies to organizational transformations. Before embarking on major changes, it's crucial to honestly assess your starting point and make sure you have the right ingredients to arrive at your destination. This involves evaluating your organization's leadership, culture, resources, whether employees are committed to the change, and more.

Reflect on Your Organizational Culture

Organizational culture is an often-invisible force that shapes the way things are done within your organization. While blanket statements should generally be avoided, it is no exaggeration to say that this force will significantly influence the success of your transformation, irrespective of your industry and the sector your organization is operating in.

As such, before kicking off your transformation journey, take a moment to honestly assess:

> **?** Does your organization foster adaptability, openness to innovation, and collaboration, or is it still stuck in old ways of doing things, resistant to change, and plagued by internal politics?

Quick Tips: Understanding Your Organizational Culture

Quick Tips

- Compare your stated values to observed behaviors. Look for the differences between what your organization claims it values and how employees are rewarded and recognized.
- Note the "hero stories" that are repeatedly told. Notice whether they focus on adaptability and innovation, or on maintaining the status quo.
- Study how people are promoted and rewarded. Pay attention to whether risk-takers who try new things and push for positive change are recognized, or if those who maintain the status quo are favored - especially if promotions seem based on personal connections rather than merit.

Scrutinize Your Organizational Structure

Think of your organization's structure as the blueprint of how your company operates. It shows how information flows and where decisions are made.

Understanding your organization's structure is crucial since it can reveal potential bottlenecks that might hinder your transformation. Keep in mind that an inflexible structure can delay quick decision making and slow down the change process. Meanwhile, a structure that promotes autonomy and quick responses will enhance the overall effectiveness of your organization.

With this in mind, starting by assessing and realigning your overall organizational structure can be a key contributing factor for boosting your transformation, especially if these realignments provide your employees the empowerment needed to support you in the change.

Quick Tips: Identifying Bottlenecks

Quick
Tips

- Choose a recent major decision and map out the process. Who was involved? How long did it take? Were there any obstacles encountered? All of these highlight potential bottlenecks.
- Follow the ways critical information, such as strategy changes and market insights, move across the organization, noting any delays or one-way communication patterns.

Study Processes and Workflows

Any work that is done follows a process - whether that process is formalized and structured or ad hoc, informal and intuitive, every piece of work that is done in your organization follows a set of steps. Evaluating these steps (processes and workflows) will not only help you understand how work is actually being done but also pinpoint areas where your processes can be streamlined or completely redefined to support your new business goals.

As a result, it is very common for effective transformations to require sometimes large changes to key processes, all to enhance overall efficiency, reduce costs, and improve customer satisfaction.

Quick Tips: Identifying Processes and Workflows

Quick
Tips

- Observe how work is actually carried out day-to-day, not how procedures are documented. Pinpoint unnecessary steps, redundancies, or innovation blockers.
- Identify where projects or tasks tend to stall when moving between teams. This reveals areas where goals or responsibilities might be misaligned.

- Ask employees to identify where they regularly waste time on low-value, repetitive tasks. This direct feedback can highlight potential areas for process improvement.

Analyze Your Technology Infrastructure

In nearly every transformation, your organization's technological infrastructure is a critical element. These are the computer systems, tools, and software on or through which work is carried out.

Evaluating your organization's technology landscape is therefore imperative to understand whether it is robust enough to support you throughout the transformation journey.

Apart from the technology itself, this assessment must include understanding whether your setup includes legacy systems that are challenging to update, build upon, or expand. Such systems can significantly hinder the transformation due to the complexities of integrating them with newer solutions.

Additionally, it's essential to consider the cultural and human factors related to these systems. You need to assess the relationship of stakeholders with the existing technology and ask:

? Are people willing to transition from systems they may have used for decades to newer solutions that require them to step out of their comfort zones and learn new skills?

Understanding this aspect is crucial because it directly affects how quickly the changes are adopted, or whether they are adopted at all, impacting the ultimate success of new technologies within your organization.

Keep in mind that this comprehensive analysis must not only identify technical gaps. It should also serve to align your technological landscape with both the strategic goals of the transformation and the capabilities of your workforce. This ensures that technology acts as an enabler rather than a barrier in your transformation journey.

Quick Tips: Strategically Analyzing Your Technology Infrastructure

Quick Tips

- Go beyond simply listing what software you have. Assess the age of both physical and software systems, their compatibility with modern solutions, ease of data extraction, and vendor support levels. This creates a holistic picture of potential roadblocks during integration.
- Tech staff know the technical issues, but frontline employees feel the daily pain points. Interview them about workarounds they've created, time wasted on outdated systems, and frustrations that the transformation could solve.
- Even the best technical solution fails if adoption is low. To avoid this, map out how proposed changes would impact people's daily workflows and identify specific skill gaps or mindsets that will need to shift for new tech to succeed.

Evaluate Employee Skills and Capabilities

While organizations often evaluate their technology by default ahead of a major transformation, the same importance is erroneously not given to assessing their workforce's current skills and capabilities.

This nonnegotiable step will help ensure you are strategically prepared, with a clear understanding of whether your existing talent aligns with the goals of the transformation. It empowers you to proactively identify skill gaps that could derail progress, enabling you to determine the necessary initiatives to upskill and reskill your workforce ahead of time. This includes making smart investments in training or hiring, ensuring resources are targeted to the areas of greatest impact.

Moreover, understanding your people means gauging their readiness for change. This insight allows you to tailor your management style, addressing potential anxieties with strategies such as tailoring communication to specific employees.

Most importantly, involving employees in this assessment fosters engagement. When they see how the transformation both aligns with and considers their own growth aspirations, they become active participants, not merely subjects.

Quick Tips: Evaluating Employee Skills and Capabilities

- Don't rely solely on existing performance reviews or outdated job descriptions. Interview managers and colleagues to get a 360° view of both an employee's tasks and strengths, potentially revealing hidden talents.
- Transformation means work will change. Look for employees who demonstrate adaptability, problem-solving, and a willingness to learn, even if their current role doesn't seem directly related to your future needs.
- Engage Employees in Self-Assessment. Asking employees to reflect on their own strengths, weaknesses, and aspirations does two important things: it gives you valuable insights and starts the process of them taking ownership of their role in the transformation.

A Word on Leadership and Change Management

While assessing each of the above areas is crucial, keep in mind that even the best-intentioned transformations can stall without strong leaders who are fully committed to the change and understand how to guide people through it. Ask yourself these tough questions:

Do your senior leaders genuinely believe in the need for change, or are they just going through the motions? Are they willing to challenge ingrained habits and make potentially difficult decisions to achieve long-term success?

Keep in mind that leaders set the tone, and their conviction is contagious. If true leadership support is lacking, building this genuine buy-in must become your top priority.

Remember, conducting a comprehensive organizational readiness assessment can be challenging. It involves confronting hard truths and may require making decisions that affect close colleagues you have worked with for years. Therefore, it is crucial to approach this assessment cautiously, constantly ensuring that you adopt a holistic approach that takes into account how the various elements are deeply interconnected. For instance, low employee morale combined with a rigid culture can significantly undermine even the most well-funded transformation project.

Keep in mind that this assessment isn't about finding faults. Instead, it should pinpoint your organization's strengths while identifying and leveraging potential obstacles to be considered before you start defining and executing your transformation.

By achieving this clarity you will be laying the foundation for a transformation journey that has greater potential to be successful and sustainable.

Key Takeaways

- *Transformation Needs a Roadmap*: Starting a major change without honest assessment is like a road trip with no map - the odds of success are low.
- *Culture Is Crucial*: An adaptable, collaborative culture is essential for your transformation's success. Rigid, change-resistant cultures can become major roadblocks.
- *Structures Matter*: Inflexible organizational structures hinder agility and decision making. Assess how your structure may slow down the change process.
- *Processes Need Revamp*: Outdated processes and workflows cause inefficiency and frustration. Transformation may hinge on streamlining and updating them.
- *Tech Is an Enabler (Or Obstacle)*: Legacy systems and resistance to new tech hold things back. Transformation might demand significant technology upgrades and addressing the human element of change.

- *Skills Drive Success*: Assessing employee skills is as important as tech assessment. Identifying skill gaps and investing in upskilling is nonnegotiable.
- *Change Management Is NOT an Afterthought*: Employee buy-in and leadership commitment are crucial from the start. Tailored approaches are key to overcoming resistance.
- *Holistic View Is Essential*: All these factors - culture, structure, tech, and so on - are interconnected. Taking a siloed approach to assessment risks major blind spots.

CHAPTER 3

Defining Your Transformation Vision

"If you don't know where you are going, you'll end up someplace else."
—Yogi Berra

Introduction: From Assessment to a Roadmap

In the previous chapter, we saw the importance of deeply assessing your organization's current state. This essential exercise is like checking your car's vital signs - oil levels, tire pressure, and so on - before setting off on a long road trip. You wouldn't risk embarking on the journey without knowing your vehicle is ready for the challenge!

Now that you have a clear visibility of where you stand and feel comfortable and energized to start the journey, it is imperative to understand the way forward - how are you going to reach your targeted destination? To achieve such clarity, you need to perform research for deep organizational insights and be able to answer these critical questions:

> **?** Where do you excel?
> What potential roadblocks need addressing?

Knowing the answers to these questions is important as these will help you define a strategic roadmap that will ultimately guide your organization toward its desired future state.

Customer-Centricity: The Heart of Your Strategy

In today's hypercompetitive landscape, a customer-centric strategy isn't just an option; it's a necessity for an organization's survival and growth.

Simply put, such a strategy means placing your customer at the heart of your transformation.

This involves understanding the customer's needs, preferences, and pain points at a deep level. Those insights will then drive every decision you make - from product development to service delivery.

Why Customer-Centricity Matters

Adopting a customer-centric approach means taking decisions that place clients first, in turn translating into a host of benefits that contribute toward the end goal for your transformation:

- *Increased Customer Loyalty and Retention*: Customers who feel understood and served by your organization will be more likely to return to your brand for their future needs. Additionally, there's also a higher chance of marketing your brand through word of mouth, a powerful method that is otherwise hard to replicate.

- *Enhanced Revenue Growth*: Such a loyal customer base translates into long-term benefits for your organization. Loyal customers have the potential to become your organization's best marketing asset, ultimately boosting your bottom line.

- *Improved Decision Making*: By understanding your customers' wants and needs, your organization can then make informed decisions about the way products are developed and marketed, along with the business' overall direction. This leads to more effective initiatives and a higher return on the investments into your transformation.

Customer-Centricity in Action

No matter the industry, those businesses that make their customer's experience a priority, reap the rewards. For instance, a clothing retailer might leverage data on their customer's preferences to offer personalized product recommendations and tailor promotions. This ultimately results in a more engaging shopping experience and increased sales.

In the financial services sector, a bank could go beyond simply processing transactions by developing a user-friendly mobile app. This app could provide customers with easy access to their finances, personalized financial advice based on their spending habits, and proactive alerts about potential issues - initiatives that foster a sense of trust and partnership.

Similarly, health care providers who place patients at the center of their services might implement online appointment scheduling, offer telehealth options for convenient consultations, and maintain clear communication channels for post-treatment care. This comprehensive focus on making the patient's experience the best that it could be can significantly improve health outcomes, foster loyalty, and encourage positive word-of-mouth referrals.

These are just a few examples of how customer-centricity can be applied across different industries. The key is to understand that "Customer-Centricity" is not a buzzword but a way to approach your business that should pervade each of your decisions. By putting the customer at the center of your transformation, you're not just making changes; you're considering your products through a customer's perspective, improving satisfaction and loyalty for a future of sustainable success.

Remember, understanding your customers is a continuous process; their needs and market trends shift over time and are not set in stone.

Powerful Tools to Gain Customer Insights

To truly understand your customer base, there are several powerful tools at your disposal. Tailored surveys offer direct insight, capturing specific feedback on client experiences, preferences, and areas for improvement. Social media analysis allows you to tap into online conversations, revealing customer sentiment and emerging industry trends.

Perhaps most insightful of all is visually mapping your customer's journey by outlining all touchpoints, from initial awareness to post-purchase interactions. This comprehensive view highlights opportunities to improve the experience and proactively address pain points, ultimately increasing customer satisfaction.

Quick Tips: Building A Customer-Centric Strategy

Quick Tips

Define the "Who"

Identify and understand the customers you aim to serve over the next few years. Use detailed personas that include demographic information such as age, sex, interests, lifestyle, and income. Personas should be made vivid and accessible throughout the organization - displayed in common areas and used in strategic discussions to maintain focus on customer needs.

Plan the "How"

Analyze how customers will interact with your products or services. This includes ensuring your technology infrastructure can support these interactions - whether they happen digitally or in person - and refining customer service processes to be more responsive and knowledgeable.

Anticipate the "What"

Determine the products or services customers will likely desire in the coming years. This involves not only meeting but anticipating future needs to create solutions that will give you the competitive edge.

Understand the "Why"

Reflect deeply on why customers would choose your offerings over competitors'. This includes leveraging any historical data and relationships to maintain loyalty and using insights to stay ahead of potential new entrants in the market.

By utilizing these tools and adopting a customer-centric mindset, you'll gain a deeper understanding of your customers, enabling you to create a compelling vision and strategy that drives long-term success for your organization.

Remember, customer-centric transformation is a continuous journey, not a checklist to complete. By regularly monitoring customer feedback and adjusting your strategies, your organization will remain agile, responsive, and laser-focused on exceeding customer expectations.

This dynamic approach ensures you'll consistently stay ahead of changing customer demands, leading to long-term success.

Defining Your "North Star"

With a deep understanding of your customers at the forefront, it's time to define the destination of your transformation - your "North Star" vision. This should be a clear, compelling long-term goal that articulates your organization's highest aspirations and provides direction for all strategic decisions and initiatives.

Defining your "North Star" is particularly crucial when your organization faces multiple challenges. This is because it ensures that you do not lose sight of your goals amid these difficulties. Moreover, a well-defined and effectively communicated North Star can ignite passion and purpose across your organization, motivating everyone to work toward a shared goal that leads to your ultimate destination.

Quick Tips: Forming Your Customer-Centric "North Star"

Quick Tips

- *Start with the Customer.* What are their deepest needs and biggest pain points? How will you transform their experience in a way that exceeds expectations?
- *Align with Core Values.* While customer-centricity is paramount, your vision should also reflect the non-negotiable principles that define your organization.
- *Paint a Vivid Picture.* Use descriptive language that inspires and illustrate the successful future state you are striving toward.
- *Be Bold and Aspirational.* Your "North Star" should represent a significant leap forward, not just incremental improvement. Dare to dream big!
- *Create Emotional Connections.* Remember, besides including technological aspirations, your vision should aim for a strong emotional connection with your customers, where they feel understood and valued by your brand.

Example of a Software Company's North Star:

"We will be the <u>indispensable</u> platform that transforms <u>complex data</u> into actionable insights, <u>empowering our customers</u> to make <u>confident, data-driven decisions</u> with unparalleled ease - all while upholding our commitment to <u>transparency and data integrity</u>."

Collaboration is key. To ensure your "North Star" resonates broadly and gains strong buy-in, make sure that key stakeholders are involved through the whole process. Gather insights from your leadership team, employees across various departments, and even trusted customers or partners. This collaborative approach ensures that your "North Star" reflects diverse perspectives and inspires wide-spread engagement.

Remember, your "North Star" is your guide, not a rigid destination. Revisit and adjust it regularly to ensure it remains aligned with evolving customer needs and market dynamics. Significant market shifts, competitor launches, or major tech innovations could all be potential triggers to re-evaluate your vision.

From Vision to Action: Developing Your Transformation Roadmap

With your "North Star" clearly defined, it's time to map out the journey toward it. Much like planning multiple stops on a long-distance trip, your organizational transformation requires setting clear intermediary goals. These goals serve as stepping stones that transform your strategic vision into a concrete action plan.

Involving your leadership team in this process is crucial - they bring expertise from various areas and help define realistic, valuable milestones. Their involvement not only aids in fine-tuning the plan but also secures their buy-in, which is essential for the success of the transformation.

Identify Intermediary Goals and Quick Wins

Begin by working with your leadership team to define intermediary goals that align with your broader vision. Focus on identifying *"quick wins"* - achievable goals that can be reached relatively quickly and will yield visible improvements. Think of them as progress markers along your roadmap, affirming that you're on the right track.

For example, if your "North Star" involves revolutionizing customer service, a viable short-term goal could be to reduce average response times by 25 percent. Milestones might include hiring additional support staff and launching a streamlined customer feedback process.

While coming up with short-term wins, keep an eye on your core internal processes. Re-designing the entire, or part of these processes could lead to significant wins, including savings on time and resources. Again, here the involvement of your leadership team becomes crucial as they can help you identify where quick wins could address existing bottlenecks or potential pain points in your processes.

Remember, contrary to the common belief, the aim of defining short-term wins is not to achieve immediate perfection but rather to make continual progress, learn from outcomes, and iterate. This approach helps foster a culture of achievement and reinforces commitment to the transformation journey.

Quick Tips: Maximize the Impact of Quick Wins

Quick Tips

- *Increase Engagement and Buy-In*: Enduring a long transformation journey without recognizing achievements can be demotivating. Celebrating success along the way boosts morale, helping everyone appreciate the value of their contributions and remain engaged with the transformation process.
- *Reflect and Learn*: Use each quick win as an opportunity to reflect on what worked well and what could be improved. This continuous learning helps smooth the transition to subsequent phases of the journey, ensuring that past mistakes are not repeated.
- *Test the Waters*: When a milestone involves a tangible deliverable, such as the launch of a new product, it provides a chance to gather feedback. This feedback is invaluable for adjusting your strategies. If customers respond negatively to a new offering, take time to understand their concerns and refine the product before moving forward.

Develop Strategic Initiatives

With your milestones clearly defined, it's time to design targeted initiatives that will drive progress toward them. These initiatives serve as a direct starting point to address specific challenges, alleviate customer pain points, and seize opportunities inspired by your "North Star," all while keeping your customer at the center of these efforts.

While defining the strategic initiatives, consider focusing on those that encompass these key concepts:

- *Process Improvements*: Can you streamline workflows, reduce redundancies, or automate tasks to improve efficiency and enhance the customer experience?

- *Technology Upgrades*: Do you need to implement new software, tools, or systems to better serve customers or support process improvements?

- *Data-Driven Decision Making*: Can you leverage analytics and data to gain better insights into your customers for better-tailored offerings?

- *Employee Training and Development*: What skills or knowledge gaps need addressing to ensure your team delivers the exceptional customer experience your vision demands?

- *Customer Engagement Strategies*: How will you proactively connect with customers, build relationships, and gather feedback to drive continuous improvement?

Note how each concept supports the end goal of an improved customer experience. By keeping your clients at the heart of your strategic initiatives, your organization can transform in a way that delivers tangible value to your customers, ultimately driving sustainable growth.

Keep in mind that strategic initiatives serve as the engine of your transformation. As such, ensure each initiative clearly supports a specific milestone for maximum impact. This will in turn contribute to your short-term goals and your ultimate "North Star" vision.

Key Takeaways

- *Assessment Is Essential*: It is crucial to understand your organization's current state (strengths, weaknesses, opportunities) before embarking on a transformation journey.
- *Customer-Centricity Is Key*: Do not view prioritizing customers' needs and experiences as a trend; it should serve as the foundation for sustainable growth and success.
- *A Clear "North Star" Guides You*: A well-defined, customer-centric vision serves to align your organization, providing direction during times of change.
- *Roadmap with Milestones*: Develop a clear roadmap with achievable intermediary goals in order to successfully track and achieve your transformation vision.
- *Quick Wins Matter*: Celebrating short-term successes boosts morale, fosters engagement, and creates a culture of achievement throughout the transformation.
- *Strategic Initiatives Fuel Progress*: Targeted initiatives that lead you to your destination while addressing customer pain points should leverage technology and improve processes.
- *Agility Is Essential*: Revisit and adjust your strategies, including your "North Star," in response to changing customer needs and market dynamics.
- *Collaboration Is Crucial*: Involve stakeholders throughout the process of defining your vision, roadmap, and initiatives. This will ensure broad buy-in and a shared understanding of the goals.

Case Study: FINxP PAYMENTS – A FINTECH TRANSFORMATION JOURNEY

(The company's name has been changed to protect its identity.)

FINxP Payments, a fintech company specializing in cross-border payments for a growing clientele of mid-sized e-commerce businesses, began facing challenges as the global e-commerce market exploded in popularity. FINxP's existing systems struggled to keep pace with the surge in transactions and the increasing complexity of international regulations.

I was engaged to develop and lead a comprehensive transformation that would allow the company to scale its operations, streamline compliance, and maintain its competitive edge in the evolving fintech landscape.

The Wake-Up Call

My first task was to assess the situation and determine the urgency for change. FINxP Payments had enjoyed early success, but now, customer frustration was mounting. Transactions were slow; fees were confusing; and new, agile fintech competitors were emerging. Internally, innovation was hindered as teams operated in silos, preventing them from keeping up with market demands.

The data backed up these concerns: increasing customer churn meant users dropped out from FINxP's services more frequently, satisfaction scores plummeted, and our market share was beginning to erode. It was clear that if we didn't transform, we risked becoming irrelevant.

Readiness Check

Before diving into a full-scale transformation, I wanted to assess the organizational readiness for change. FINxP Payments had a few key strengths: a passionate team, a loyal customer base, and deep expertise in cross-border payments. However, some significant weaknesses were holding us back:

- *Technical Debt*: While FINxP Payments had innovated in many areas, their core transaction processing platform was held back by an aging, on-premises system that couldn't handle the new demands.

- *Compliance Labyrinth*: The ever-evolving regulatory landscape made manual compliance tracking time-consuming and risky, becoming a drain on resources.

- *Data Disconnect*: Lack of real-time data analytics hindered our ability to understand customer behavior, personalize offerings, and quickly identify potential fraud risks.

Defining Our Transformation Roadmap

With input from key stakeholders, we embarked on a collaborative strategy definition process where we conducted workshops, facilitated discussions, and closely analyzed fintech disruptors.

This intensive exploration yielded our transformative "North Star": "*Become the Global Operating System for Mid-Sized Business E-commerce.*" This vision went beyond simply processing payments. We aimed to empower our clients' growth through seamless transactions, valuable insights, and integrated financial tools. This broader vision would not only improve our core service but also position FINxP Payments as a strategic partner for our mid-sized e-commerce clientele.

Developing Strategic Initiatives:
The Path to the North Star

To achieve our North Star, our ambitious vision was broken down into smaller, actionable steps through a roadmap. We identified a series of strategic initiatives that would address the key challenges and opportunities we had identified during our readiness assessment, including those related to:

- *Customer Experience*: We committed to developing a new mobile app that would simplify cross-border payments, implementing a 24/7 multilingual customer support chatbot for instant assistance and reduced response times, and creating a simpler pricing structure with transparent fees and no hidden costs.

- *Technological Innovation*: By moving the core transaction processing platform to a cloud-based solution, we would increase scalability and reliability. Additionally, we committed investments into real-time analytics tools to monitor transactions, identify fraud and personalize customer offers. Finally, developing API integrations with popular e-commerce platforms would streamline the payment process for merchants.

- *Compliance and Risk Management*: We aimed to implement AI-powered regulatory technology solutions to automate compliance checks and ensure adherence to evolving regulations. We would also develop a robust fraud detection system that leverages machine learning, and create a centralized risk management dashboard to monitor key metrics and identify potential risks in real time.

With these strategic initiatives as our guideposts, we had laid the groundwork for our transformation. Now that the challenges had been identified, and alongside a compelling vision for the organizations future, the stage had been set for innovation. But recognizing the need for change and defining a roadmap was just the first step of the journey.

The real work was about to begin, as we now had to tackle the human side of transformation, aligning our culture and leadership with this new direction.

Explore Further

Ancillary questions and supporting materials related to this case study are available to help you apply the concepts introduced in this stage. These resources can be accessed through the QR code provided in the Preface section.

STAGE 2

Harmonize

CHAPTER 4

Planning for Transformation Success

"Plans are nothing; planning is everything."
—Dwight D. Eisenhower

Introduction: From Roadmap to an Adaptable Plan

Now that you have thoroughly reflected on your current state (the "As Is," discussed in Chapter 2) and envisioned where you want your organization to be in the future (the "To Be," discussed in Chapter 3), you likely have a deeper understanding of why transformation is necessary.

Although achieving your vision may seem challenging from your current standpoint; by engaging in these self-assessments and strategic reflections, you have laid a strong foundation for your transformation journey.

You have now reached a critical point in this journey. With the insights you've gained so far, you must identify the elements that need alignment to successfully implement an organization-wide change. Only through such alignment can you ensure a smooth and effective transition from your current state and aspirations to concrete results.

Analyzing the Gap

As seen earlier, we first developed a deeper understanding of your organization's current state. This was followed up with the creation of a clearly defined vision for the future.

Now it's time to analyze the gaps between where you are and where you want to be. Known as "gap analysis," this critical step will help you in work prioritization, resource allocation, and the development of your transformation strategy.

Bridging Assessment and Vision

Remember, your initial "As-Is" assessment and "To-Be" vision are not set in stone. The process of gap analysis itself will likely uncover new insights. This means you need to be prepared to:

1. *Reassess the Current State*: Areas where your initial "As-Is" understanding was incomplete, requiring further data collection or process mapping.

2. *Refine the Future Vision*: Aspects of your desired future state that may need adjustment based on resource constraints, organizational capabilities, or evolving market conditions.

While doing this assessment, keep an open mindset to revisiting and refining previous work. A more accurate understanding of both your start and endpoints enables a more realistic and achievable roadmap. This iterative process is crucial to driving a successful transformation.

Key Areas for Gap Analysis

To ensure a comprehensive analysis, consider these four key areas where gaps can significantly impede your transformation progress:

- Culture gaps
- Process gaps
- Technology gaps
- Capability gaps

While we'll examine these gaps separately, understand they are often deeply interconnected. For instance, a process gap might reveal that you need new technology and the skills to use it. Identifying these overlaps is key to developing holistic solutions.

Culture Gaps

Aligning your organizational culture with your "To-Be" vision is essential for sustainable transformation. Mismatches in values, decision-making processes, or the ingrained ways of operating can derail even the best-laid plans.

Culture gaps manifest in several ways: resistance to change, siloed thinking, risk aversion, a reluctance to embrace data-driven decision making, and a lack of customer-centricity.

These hinder ongoing improvement and innovation, slowing your transformation or even causing it to fail. A typical scenario, which I have encountered several times in my career, involves traditional hierarchical decision making and strict adherence to existing processes. Such ways of working prevent swift responses to market changes, despite having a "To-Be" vision that prioritizes agility.

To uncover these gaps ask yourself:

> Do your employees prefer maintaining the status quo?
>
> Is your organization's management a good model for the adaptability, collaboration, and innovation you expect of the wider organization?
>
> Does your structure and communication style allow for the agility and cross-functional collaboration your transformation hinges upon?
>
> Does your organization readily share information and knowledge across teams, or is there a silo mentality hindering effective collaboration?
>
> Are employees encouraged to experiment and take calculated risks, or is there a strong emphasis on avoiding failure at all costs?

Understanding these gaps allows you to pre-emptively manage any resistance to change, reshape communication norms, and adjust governance structures to ones that better align with your long-term goals.

However, addressing cultural gaps requires sustained effort and strategic patience. If you rush transformation initiatives without adequately addressing these foundational gaps, you risk jeopardizing the entire transformation process. Instead, maximize your transformation's feasibility and sustainability by including these considerations into the way you prioritize your initiatives and allocate resources.

Process Gaps

Process gaps refer to discrepancies between current operational procedures and the optimized, streamlined workflows needed to achieve your "To-Be" vision. If left unaddressed, these gaps could sabotage your transformation, preventing you from becoming an agile, efficient organization that is able to adapt to new challenges and meet evolving market demands effectively.

Process gaps show up as work-stalling bottlenecks, redundancies, manual steps prone to error, or overly complex approval chains. Such gaps lead to higher costs, slow down your time-to-market, frustrate customers, and disengage employees. For example, in manufacturing, outdated production scheduling processes often result in missed deadlines or inefficient use of resources.

Ask yourself these questions to pinpoint your process gaps:

> **?** Could you easily create a visual map of your core operational processes? If not, consider this a sign for areas for improvement.
> Where do you consistently observe delays, customer complaints, or errors?
> Is your process improvement mainly reactive (fixing problems as they arise) or proactive (improving things even if they are "working," to achieve greater efficiency)?

Addressing process gaps requires a methodical approach that ensures effectiveness by consulting all relevant stakeholders, improving buy-in in due course. This key change management strategy, supported by regular training sessions and clear communication to help staff understand new procedures and the benefits they bring, will facilitate the transition from old processes, to new and optimized workflows.

Technology Gaps

For your "To-Be" plan to be realized, you must ensure that your technology infrastructure:

- allows for agility.
- leverages data-driven insights for your staff.
- delivers a seamless experience.

Ensuring this means identifying discrepancies between the technological resources currently available in comparison to the ones needed to achieve your strategic objectives.

Common technology gaps may include outdated software, scattered or inadequately integrated data, limited analytics capabilities, or digital customer-facing tools that fail to meet user expectations. All of these can obstruct your ability to adapt quickly, preventing you from offering personalized experiences, or accessing the real-time insights necessary for competitive positioning.

In the health care sector, for instance, scattered patient record systems and a lack of data sharing between providers can lead to inefficiencies, in turn resulting in compromised patient care. Such gaps can be addressed through strategic upgrades that may include software improvements, cloud platform investments, or enhanced system integration - crucial factors for maintaining industry relevance.

Consider the following questions to guide your analysis:

> Are your organization's current technological systems able and integrated enough to support your desired future state?
>
> Do outdated legacy systems or data silos prevent you from gaining real-time insights into your organization? Is a lack of integration leading to missed insights?
>
> Are your technological systems designed to support processes that are themselves outdated?
>
> Do your customer-facing tools match the ease and personalization customers expect based on their experiences with industry leaders?

Given the importance of technology in the operations of any contemporary organization, your transformation will depend heavily on technological advancements and considerations. Nevertheless, you must meticulously plan the introduction of any new technology to avoid or minimize disruptions to existing workflows. Additionally, you must also ensure your team has the required skills to make the best use of it.

Accurately understanding and addressing these technology gaps in relation to your strategic initiatives is vital for effectively planning and executing your transformation.

Capability Gaps

Analyzing process and technology gaps often reveals that your team may lack the skills, knowledge, or mindset to fully realize the potential of your "To-Be" vision. These capability gaps are a major obstacle to your transformation, leading to slow implementation or suboptimal results, even with upgraded processes and tools.

Remember that these gaps can take different forms and shapes. There might be gaps in technical capabilities (not enough developers with cloud expertise), process-oriented capabilities (lack of Lean methodology skills for optimization), leadership abilities (lack of experience managing distributed teams), or even gaps in the broader mindsets (lack of adaptability and openness to learning).

For example, in a company pivoting toward AI-driven offerings, not only is data science expertise essential, but there is also a broader need for upskilling the entire team to ensure effective collaboration. Similarly, in the retail sector, a salesforce proficient only in in-person interactions may struggle to deliver the personalized digital experience that modern customers expect.

Consider these questions to identify capability gaps:

> **?** Do you have the necessary in-house expertise to innovate, adapt, and manage the technological upgrades required during your transformation?
> How well-prepared is your leadership team to drive a culture change, potentially requiring them to learn new management styles?

Are your training and development programs focused on the skills essential for realizing your "To-Be" vision, or mainly on maintaining existing competencies and ways of working?

Are you prepared to strategically supplement your existing talent through new hires or partnerships to ensure access to all the expertise your transformation journey demands?

Remember, capability development is an ongoing process that complements your broader transformation. Understanding your capability gaps is not merely about identifying deficits; it's about empowering your team for successful transformation. As your organization evolves, new technologies will emerge, and customer expectations will shift. Consequently, your transformation plan should be viewed as a living document, one that adapts through continuous learning and upskilling, flexible management practices, and proactive talent management.

Tools for Gap Analysis

While the core principles of gap analysis are straightforward, there are various tools and frameworks that can add structure and depth to your analysis. These range from simple visual aids to more complex methodologies.

Popular choices include comparative mapping (visualizing "As-Is" and "To-Be" organizational states to easily identify discrepancies), customer journey mapping (understanding gaps from the customer's perspective), and benchmarking against industry leaders to identify areas where you may be lagging. Additionally, frameworks such as the SWOT analysis (Strengths, Weaknesses, Opportunities, Threats) can offer a broader perspective of the factors that could impact your transformation.

Experimenting with different tools can be valuable - the key is finding what works best to reveal the specific insights that will guide your strategic refinements and prioritization decisions.

Refining Your Transformation Roadmap

A thorough gap analysis doesn't just reveal areas for improvement - it provides the crucial data you need to refine the initiatives outlined in Chapter 3, creating a roadmap with a significantly higher chance of success.

At this stage, take a moment and look back at your strategic initiatives in conjunction with the gaps you have identified. This analysis could reveal several important adjustments, including:

1. *New Strategic Initiatives*: You might discover that certain gaps are so critical they require dedicated initiatives to address them. For example, a major culture gap hindering innovation may necessitate a focused initiative on change management and the development of collaborative mindsets. Similarly, discovering a lack of data analytics skills might necessitate adding upskilling initiatives before embarking into AI-driven projects outlined in your "To-Be" vision.

2. *Scope Adjustments*: In some cases, the analysis might reveal gaps larger than anticipated for certain initiatives. If so, consider reducing the scope or breaking initiatives into more manageable phases for greater feasibility.

3. *Removal of Strategic Initiative*: Sometimes, a gap may be so substantial that it merits a dedicated transformation effort in its own right. In such instances, it may be prudent to remove this target from your immediate "North Star" objectives to concentrate on more achievable ones.

By refining your strategic initiatives in light of the gap analysis, you proactively address obstacles and ensure your efforts are truly aligned with the actions needed to reach your "North Star." Remember, this is an ongoing process - as your organization transforms, new gaps will emerge, necessitating continuous adjustments as part of your strategic management approach.

Prioritizing for Impact

A common challenge in organizational change is the desire to tackle all initiatives at once. While enthusiasm is admirable, trying to address too many things simultaneously can lead to overwhelmed teams, scattered resources, and stalled progress. This makes prioritization an essential component for keeping your transformation focused and efficient.

Visualizing the Strategy

Using the potential strategic initiatives identified in the previous chapter, begin by laying out all strategic initiatives in a high-level timeline format, together with their short- and long-term benefits. At this stage, avoid delving too deeply into the duration of each initiative; the goal is to visualize where these initiatives fit within the larger scheme of your transformation journey.

The Right Moves in the Right Order: Sequencing for Success

With a visual map in hand, it becomes easier to sequence your initiatives. Identify the dependencies between them to ensure maximal efficiency. You should also look at possible synergies that could allow you to group initiatives into one, keeping teams focused on deliverables. This strategic sequencing is akin to planning a holiday itinerary that flows logically from start to destination, avoiding backtracking and inefficiencies.

Beyond the Obvious ...

When evaluating the sequence and feasibility of initiatives, consider other factors such as governance frameworks, policies, and technology infrastructure limitations. These elements can impact the execution and timing of your planned initiatives, influencing the sequence in which they should be deployed.

Evaluating and Prioritizing Initiatives

Now, with all initiatives laid out and sequenced, assess each one based on several critical factors to prioritize effectively. While prioritizing, for each initiative ask yourself the following:

- *Alignment*: How strongly does the initiative support milestone achievement and your "North Star"?

- *Customer Impact*: Will it deliver tangible improvements to the customer experience?

- *ROI and Feasibility*: What's the potential return, and do you have the resources to implement it successfully? While ROI shouldn't be the sole determining factor, it's crucial for initiatives requiring substantial resource investment.

- *Risk and Mitigation*: What are potential risks, and how can these be proactively addressed? Higher-risk initiatives might require more preparation or could be scheduled later in the transformation process.

- *Competitive Advantage*: Could the initiative give you an edge in your industry? These can be critical in industries where technological or service differentiation is a key driver of success.

- *Cross-Functional Benefits*: Does it positively impact multiple areas of your business?

**Quick Tips:
Prioritization Mechanisms**

Quick Tips

To strategically prioritize your initiatives, consider various prioritization mechanisms. The best choice depends on the nature of your initiatives, available information, and industry-specific factors. The following are some of the most frequent prioritization mechanisms I have used.

WEIGHTED SCORING

Description: Assign numerical scores to each initiative based on prioritization factors that are applicable to your situation, like for instance Strategic Alignment, Customer Impact, and ROI. You can customize factors and weigh them according to your organization's specific priorities. The total score helps determine an initiative's relative importance.

Application: Use this method to compare initiatives objectively, reducing bias. It's particularly helpful when evaluating a large number of potential initiatives.

Benefits: Provides a transparent and justifiable method for prioritization. Given the factor-specific scoring system, it is highly adaptable and flexible through score and weighting adjustments.

Challenges: Weighted scoring models require careful consideration when being developed. Selecting which factors to include or discard, and how heavily to weigh them for accurate ranking can be a complex, data-intensive, and significant undertaking.

MoSCoW

Description: MoSCoW ranking works by categorizing initiatives into four groups: Must Have, Should Have, Could Have, and Won't Have. Using this method, teams can more easily prioritize between essential and nice-to-have initiatives, avoiding the temptation of taking up initiatives that may be more exciting than others but less critical.

Application: Use this method when you need clear differentiation between what is critical for immediate success and what can be delayed without significant impact. It is especially useful in projects with tight deadlines or limited resources.

Benefits: Simplifies decision making by clarifying the level of necessity for each initiative. It also ensures that crucial tasks get the focus and resources they need.

Challenges: Categorizing tasks into the four categories can be a subjective process, leading to inconsistencies and biases. This is exacerbated if clear criteria are not established. There is also a risk of prioritizing immediate, short-term needs at the expense of long-term strategic goals.

KANO MODEL

Description: The Kano Model classifies initiatives or features based on how they impact customer satisfaction: Must-Be (basic expectations), Performance (linear satisfaction), and Delighters (unexpected positives).

Application: Use this model to gain a customer-centric perspective on prioritization. It helps ensure you're investing in features that will truly drive satisfaction and helps identify potential areas for innovation based on "Delighters."

Benefits: Helps organizations prioritize based on direct impact on customer satisfaction, ensuring that development efforts are aligned with creating value that customers will appreciate and pay for.

Challenges: Customer preferences can change over time, making it difficult to maintain the accuracy of categorizations. What may be considered an attractive quality today could become a must-have in the future.

Tools for Strategic Planning and Prioritization

In addition to these techniques, consider using tools to visualize and manage the complex information involved in prioritization. For example, project management software often includes features for timeline creation and dependency mapping, and some even have built-in scoring systems.

Mind-mapping tools can also be helpful for visually brainstorming initiatives and potential connections between them. If you want even more specialized support, there's dedicated prioritization software that incorporates various models and offers comparison matrices. Remember, even basic spreadsheets for scoring or diagramming software for dependencies can be highly effective.

Agility Is Key: Embracing Change as a Constant

Keep in mind that prioritization is an ongoing process. As your transformation progresses, it is essential to continuously reassess and reprioritize initiatives based on current conditions, market dynamics, and achieved outcomes. This dynamic approach ensures that your transformation remains agile and strategically aligned.

Additionally, maintain a log of initiatives that were not initially prioritized. These records can be invaluable as they may become relevant and useful at different stages of your transformation journey, allowing for flexibility in response to changing circumstances.

Aligning Resources with Your Goals

With your goals, milestones, and prioritized strategic initiatives clearly defined, it's time to strategically assess the diverse resources required to achieve your transformation vision. Ensuring adequate resources at every stage increases the chance that you remain on track during your transformation journey. At this stage it is worth considering:

- *Human Resources*: Go beyond simply identifying headcount needs. Assess the specific skills, expertise, and leadership capabilities required for each initiative. Consider different levels of the organization, from operational staff to executive leadership, to ensure comprehensive coverage.

- *Technological Resources*: Determine the technological tools, software, and systems necessary to support each initiative. This may include the need for new technologies that facilitate innovation, enhance productivity, or streamline processes.

- *Financial Resources*: Develop a high-level budget that reflects the cost of each initiative - from technology and personnel to potential external engagements. This budget should incorporate all capital needed to fund the transformation and align with your strategic priorities.

- *Time and Scheduling*: Account for potential bottlenecks, such as limited personnel with specialized skills, the time needed for training on new systems, and any external dependencies that could impact your schedule.

- *Physical Resources*: Don't overlook potential needs for additional workspace, equipment upgrades, or facility modifications depending on your industry and initiatives. Assess these early in the process to ensure they are incorporated into your budget and planning.

- *Informational Resources*: Successful transformations require data, market insights, and industry-specific knowledge. Outline the information needed by your organization and identify the ways in which it can be sourced. This could include in-house data analysis, market research, or consultation with experts.

- *Strategic Partnerships*: Some resource gaps require collaborations with external entities, such as suppliers, vendors, industry associations or research institutions. Collaborations can accelerate delivery, gain access to specialized knowledge, or facilitate entry into new markets.

Remember, resource assessment shouldn't be done in isolation for each initiative. Strive for an overarching view of the resources needed at each stage of your transformation. This holistic approach ensures feasibility, reveals potential synergies, and highlights any areas where adjustments may be needed.

Identifying and planning for resource needs throughout the transformation journey is critical to ensure that all initiatives are properly supported from start to finish. By clearly understanding the resource demands at each phase, you can ensure that each step of the transformation is feasible and aligned with your strategic goals.

This proactive approach to resource planning facilitates a smooth transformation process, tailored to achieve the "North Star" with optimal efficiency and effectiveness.

Measuring Progress

With strategic priorities established and resources aligned, defining clear metrics of success is essential. Without a defined way to track progress, your stakeholders may misinterpret goals, problems can go undetected until it's too late, and your team's motivation may wane as wins go unnoticed and uncelebrated.

The Power of SMART Goals

SMART goals allow for your organization's aspirations to be turned into realistic targets. This acronym ensures your goals are:

- *(S) Specific*: Clearly define what you want to achieve, avoiding vague or ambiguous objectives.
- *(M) Measurable*: Include quantifiable metrics to track progress and determine success.
- *(A) Achievable*: While goals should be ambitious, they should also be achievable with the resources and constraints at hand. Unattainable goals can demoralize your team and derail the transformation process.
- *(R) Relevant*: Ensure each goal directly supports your overall transformation vision and strategic initiatives.
- *(T) Time-bound*: Establish specific deadlines to create a sense of urgency and accountability.

SMART goals prevent misinterpretation and ensure everyone is aligned on how progress will be measured, reducing the risk of your transformation going off course. While there is a lot of literature available on the details of setting SMART goals, let's look at some key examples of real-life SMART goals I've used in three different industries to further illustrate their power:

Examples:

- Manufacturing:
  - ○ Vague Goal: Reduce production defects.
  - ○ SMART Goal: Reduce the product defect rate by 20 percent within the next six months, as measured by quality control data.
- Health care:
  - ○ Vague Goal: Improve patient outcomes.
  - ○ SMART Goal: Reduce the readmission rate for cardiac patients by 10 percent within the next year.

- Retail:
  - Vague Goal: Increase online sales.
  - SMART Goal: Grow e-commerce revenue by 15 percent over the next quarter, prioritizing mobile purchases.

OKRs: A Framework for Ambitious Transformations

Objectives and Key Results (OKRs) are another powerful goal-setting framework that can be particularly useful if your organization's environment requires rapid innovation and adaptation. OKRs differ from SMART goals in a few key areas:

- *Stretch Goals*: OKRs encourage setting highly ambitious, even seemingly unattainable objectives. The idea is to push the boundaries of what's possible.

- *Moonshot Thinking*: While SMART goals focus on achievable targets, OKRs accommodate the "moonshot" mentality, where achieving even 70 percent of an objective is considered a success.

- *Frequent Iteration*: OKRs are often set on shorter cycles (quarterly) compared to SMART goals, promoting agility and responsiveness to change.

With the concept of *Stretch Goals, Moonshot Thinking*, and *Frequent Iteration*, the OKR framework is the right tool for you to push your organization toward embracing adaptability and agility especially if you are operating in a fast-paced or rapidly evolving industry.

Always keep in mind that your transformation won't follow a perfectly straight line. Goals, OKRs, and KPIs must be regularly revisited as your initiatives take shape and market conditions evolve.

Additionally, make sure that you and your team are willing to embrace data as a tool for continuous improvement and course correction as it's the key to ensuring your transformation not only achieves its goals, but exceeds expectations.

Quick Tips: Use Key Performance Indicators (KPIs) to Track What Matters

Quick
Tips

Key performance indicators (KPIs) are the quantifiable metrics that can measure progress toward both the SMART goals and OKR frameworks. When choosing KPIs, consider:

Leading Versus Lagging Indicators
Leading indicators are metrics that help project future outcomes (e.g., website traffic, customer inquiries), while lagging indicators reflect your past performance (e.g., sales revenue, churn rate). Use a combination of both to get a comprehensive picture of your progress.

Financial Versus Operational
Include financial metrics (revenue, profitability, costs), but also track operational KPIs that directly impact your transformation goals and overall customer experience (response times, defect rates, employee engagement).

Relevance to Transformation Goals
Ensure your KPIs are directly linked to your strategic initiatives and overall "North Star." Clearly establish benchmarks and targets to provide a basis for comparison, helping you assess whether you are on track.

Data Systems
Have processes in place to collect, analyze, and report on your KPI data regularly. This may involve new software tools, process changes, and establishing clear roles and responsibilities for data management.

Key Takeaways

- *Transformation Success Hinges on Accurate Self-Assessment*: A thorough gap analysis revealing both strengths and weaknesses provides a realistic foundation for planning.
- *Plans Must Be Adaptable*: The insights gained from analyzing your organization's "As-Is" and the "To-Be" states may necessitate adjustments to your initial strategic roadmap.
- *Prioritization Is Essential*: Transformation involves many potential initiatives. Focus on those with the highest impact, greatest feasibility, and strongest alignment with your overall goals.

- *Aligning Resources with Transformation Goals Is Critical*: This includes financial, human, technological, and informational resources needed to support your initiatives and drive change.
- *Adaptability Is Non-negotiable*: Plans will change. Market shifts, learnings from your initiatives, and evolving technologies require a mindset of continuous adjustment and a data-driven approach to decision making.

CHAPTER 5

Building a Culture of Change

"Culture eats strategy for breakfast."

—Peter Drucker

Introduction: Building an Adaptable Culture

Picture this: two established companies within your industry. One clings to a formula that has yielded success so far, hesitant to change anything that "seems to be working." The other recognizes that even current success is no guarantee of future relevance. They constantly question, experiment, and refine their ways of working.

A decade from now, which company is more likely to not just survive but lead your industry?

Transformation is not about keeping your technology landscape up to date with the latest trends. It's about developing a culture across your organization where continuous improvement, resilience, and a willingness to learn, become your natural way of working.

That said, when it comes to transformation, culture is the difference between achieving your North Star and falling frustratingly short.

The Mindset Shift for Success: From Fear to Opportunity

Psychologist Carol Dweck's research has demonstrated how our mindset - i.e., how we perceive ourselves and the world around us - deeply shapes our reactions to challenges and opportunities for growth.

Fixed Mindset: Finding Excuses, Not Solutions

This perspective sees talents and abilities as static, inherent traits that are unchangeable. Individuals with a fixed mindset tend to view mistakes as indicators of personal failures and evidence of their limitations.

They might avoid challenges or give up easily when faced with obstacles, perceiving effort as futile because they believe "you either have it or you don't." Additionally, they often feel threatened by the success of others, seeing it as a benchmark against which they fall short.

In a workplace dominated by fixed mindsets, transformation initiatives are likely to meet significant resistance. Individuals may focus more on why changes cannot be implemented, rather than exploring innovative solutions or alternatives.

> **?** Think about how your team typically responds to setbacks. Do they focus on blame, or on finding solutions?

Growth Mindset: Embracing the Journey

Conversely, a growth mindset embraces the possibility of development and learning. It operates on the principle that skills can be honed through persistence and effort. Those with a growth mindset view mistakes as valuable learning opportunities, essential for growth and improvement.

Challenges are seen not as threats but as opportunities to learn, innovate, and develop resilience, making this crucial in transformations where people will be asked to move out of their traditional way of working/comfort zone into something new.

The Challenge of Creating a Change-Ready Culture

Let's be honest: While it's essential to have a growth mindset for a successful transformation, fostering it across your organization is no easy feat.

During the initial phases of transformation, failures may be more frequent, particularly as your team navigates through cultural shifts. This is where it gets tough. Unless you and your leadership team consistently set the right example, there's a real risk that individuals might revert to their traditional ways of working. Ask yourself,

> **?** How long has it been since you've stepped outside your comfort
> zone to learn a new skill? What about taking on a challenge you
> weren't sure you could overcome? How can you make this visible
> to your team to encourage them to do the same?

Promoting a growth mindset involves continuous encouragement and reinforcement from all levels of management. You must model this mindset by openly engaging with challenges, demonstrating perseverance, and learning from setbacks. By consistently modeling a growth mentality, you gradually build a more flexible, innovative, and resilient workforce.

Quick Tips

Quick Tips: Building A Growth Mindset Across Your Organization

- *Embrace Challenges Openly*: Tackle tough problems head-on as this signals to team members that setbacks are learning opportunities, not failures.
- *Talk About Your Learning*: Share a time you pushed outside your comfort zone, perhaps mastering a new skill or changing how you approach a task. This demonstrates that everyone can develop.
- *Own Your Mistakes*: Instead of deflecting blame, focus on, "What can we learn to prevent this in the future?" This shows that it's safe for others to admit imperfection.
- *Celebrate Process Milestones*: Recognize team members who took risks, even if the project itself didn't hit every target. This reinforces that the journey is important.
- *Highlight "Lessons Learned"*: Hold debriefs where the focus isn't on finding fault, but on what insights can be applied going forward.
- *Reframe Failure*: If a project flops completely, ask "What did we learn about our process, or our assumptions, that will lead to success next time?"
- *Offer Learning Opportunities*: Provide access to workshops, online courses, or mentorship programs, making skill development a normal part of work.

- *Encourage Cross-Team Knowledge Sharing*: Set up "lunch and learn" sessions where employees teach each other, normalizing the idea that expertise can be gained from peers.
- *Tie Growth to Advancement*: During reviews, don't limit discussions to results but rather consider what the employee is actively doing to learn and improve.
- *Delegate with Trust*: Allow team members to take calculated risks, knowing you support their decision making even if the outcome isn't ideal.
- *Ask "What if . . ." Questions*: Instead of immediately outlining a solution, encourage employees to brainstorm out-of-the-box approaches.
- *Recognize Those Who Embrace the Mindset*: Publicly praise employees who proactively seek feedback, step outside their comfort zone, or readily adapt to change.

Remember that market dynamics and customer behavior will continue to change, which makes it harder for you to harmonize between your organization's transformation and its shifting operational environment. Ensure that you invest in developing a culture where continuous improvement becomes ingrained in your organization's DNA.

Ritualizing Change

We've discussed the importance of shifting from fixed to growth mindsets within your organization. Yet, even when individuals embrace change, there's the danger of backsliding into old habits. While senior management may deliver speeches on the, sometimes perceived, success of the organizational transformation journey, grand speeches or one-off training sessions will do more harm than good.

Employees, especially those who are heavily involved in the changes, will notice the gaps between what is happening on a daily basis and theses verbal messages and will lose trust in the leaders. Most of the time they also become more disengaged to contribute to the changes.

On the contrary, true change happens when you embed new habits that reinforce adaptability as the norm. This means a relentless focus on continuous improvement, proactively learning from past successes and failures, celebrating progress, and making the impact of your transformation efforts tangible.

Remember, that your employees are your biggest asset in this journey. Their enthusiasm and willingness to adapt are crucial for success, which makes investing in their development and engagement a powerful driver of your transformation's success.

> **?** But do your leaders possess the right traits to effectively guide their teams in initiating and sustaining change?

Key Takeaways

- *Transformation Requires a Culture Shift*: It's not enough to update technology; true transformation means fostering a culture of continuous improvement, resilience, and a willingness to learn.
- *Mindset Matters*: An organization dominated by fixed mindsets will struggle to adapt, while growth mindsets are essential for embracing change as an opportunity.
- *Change Is Constant*: Market dynamics and customer needs will continue to evolve. To sustain transformation, continuously improving and adapting isn't optional, but essential.
- *Rituals Reinforce*: One-off events won't create lasting change. Embedding rituals that emphasize learning from the past, celebrating progress, and sharing knowledge are crucial for making adaptability the norm.
- *Employees Are Key*: Employee enthusiasm and willingness to embrace change are essential for transformation success. Investing in their continuous development and engagement is a powerful driver, not just a cost.
- *Leaders Set the Tone*: Successfully fostering a growth mindset requires leaders to model the desired behaviors, demonstrating openness to challenges, learning from mistakes, and celebrating the development journey.

Case Study: Microsoft's Cultural Transformation

In the early 2010s, innovative tech giant Microsoft found itself at a crossroads. Its once-vibrant organizational culture was now plagued with internal competition and resistance to new ideas. This poor mentality meant Microsoft lost its ability to adapt to a market it once dominated.

Satya Nadella - The Visionary CEO

As soon as he became Microsoft's CEO in 2014, Satya Nadella prioritized cultural change within the company, focusing on a more agile and customer-centric organization.

Nadella worked to introduce the growth mindset at Microsoft. He turned his employees' "know-it-alls" culture into a "learn-it-alls" mindset that prioritized continuous learning, collaboration, and openness to embrace new challenges. This ultimately led to a more adaptable and resilient workforce.

Nadella made sure to actively model the behaviors he wanted to see. He openly acknowledged his own shortcomings, actively sought feedback from others, and championed empathy within the organization.

Through his efforts, psychological safety was prioritized within the organization. This meant it became a space where employees felt comfortable taking risks and experimenting. Failure was seen as a learning opportunity rather than a career-ending mistake.

In what has now become an infamous move, he encouraged his leadership team to read Marshall B. Rosenberg's book *Nonviolent Communication* with the aim of fostering better understanding and collaboration within the company.

The Result

Nadella's leadership and cultural transformation ultimately led to lasting improvements for Microsoft. These included soaring stock prices, improved employee morale, and a regaining of the company's position as a market leader.

Following Nadella's changes, Microsoft launched Microsoft Teams and Azure, new and highly successful products. The company also took on a strategic partnership with Linux - a direct competitor with whom collaboration would've been unthinkable under the old culture.

Microsoft also gained financially since Nadella became CEO. Its market capitalization increased by over 500 percent. The company's performance following Nadella's changes shows the power of revitalizing an organization with a culture that empowers its employees and prioritizes customers.

Microsoft's transformation following Nadella's cultural changes truly exemplifies the power of transformations driven by empathetic leadership and a shared vision for the future. The changes underscore that the success of a culture shift isn't determined solely by a visionary CEO, but by empowering leaders at all levels to foster a culture that embraces growth, innovation, and customer-centricity.

CHAPTER 6

Leading The Change

"If your actions inspire others to dream more, learn more, do more, and become more, you are a leader."

—John Quincy Adams

Introduction: From Mindset to Leadership Action

In the previous chapter, we emphasized the importance of fostering a growth mindset across your organization. However, in the same way that a dedicated football team requires a skilled coach to guide them to victory, employees equipped with the right mindset need strong leadership to successfully navigate transformation.

This chapter introduces the concept of the "change leader" - a leader who goes beyond the nuts and bolts of implementing new processes or technologies. Instead, they give equal (or sometimes even greater) importance to inspiring their teams to embrace the unknown.

Understanding Transformational Leadership

The role of the leadership team during transformations goes far beyond just setting directives and monitoring progress. In the past, strong management skills may have been sufficient to lead an organization but during times of significant change, those skills alone are not enough. These journeys are usually long, filled with unexpected challenges, and potentially emotionally turbulent for employees, requiring strong leadership to ensure that changes are implemented, and sustained successfully.

Think of it this way: traditional managers focus on maintaining the status quo, optimizing existing processes, and ensuring things run smoothly. Change leaders, on the other hand, must ensure that the business keeps on running while motivating teams to step outside their comfort zones, and continually communicating about the greater purpose behind the disruption.

This means the leaders who are responsible for guiding your transformation need to excel in two key areas:

Strategic Leadership

Your leaders must be both the architects and the communicators of the transformation.

To guide the organization successfully, they must clearly articulate why the change is necessary and paint a compelling picture of the positive future it will create. Even when facing uncertainty, they need to set strategic priorities, allocate resources thoughtfully, and make the key decisions that drive progress. Additionally, they need to understand that transformation cannot happen in isolation.

Your organization's leaders must actively work to break down silos and encourage collaboration and unity of purpose across the organization.

Transformational Leadership

Beyond the strategic aspects, your leadership team must also focus on the human side of change.

This means proactively helping teams overcome obstacles beyond their control, streamlining processes where possible or escalating issues that require broader intervention. Recognizing that transformation is emotionally demanding, your leaders need to maintain morale through effective communication, empathy, and ongoing support.

By regularly celebrating milestones along the way, they help employees see that their contributions truly matter.

While these strategic and human-focused leadership skills are essential, another important factor sets truly effective change leaders apart from the rest.

> **?** Are your leaders vulnerable, adaptable, and visionary enough to guide your organization through successful transformation?

The Change Leader: Leading with Vulnerability, Adaptability, Vision, and Action

While there should be no single checklist of "change leader" traits, there are core qualities that differentiate those who guide their teams through transformations effectively, from those who merely manage tasks within a changing environment. Let's explore a few of the most essential:

The Power of Vulnerability

When thinking of the stereotypical "strong leader," it can be easy to assume that they must project an image of someone who has all the answers.

However, during times of transformation, vulnerability is a surprising strength.

When leaders admit they don't know exactly how things will unfold, it paradoxically allows employees to trust them more. The capability to be vulnerable with employees shows they aren't focused on appearing perfect but on finding the best path forward, together with their team.

By sharing their own stumbles, powerfully vulnerable leaders create a safe space for others to experiment and learn, knowing that setbacks are a normal part of the process. A leader who says, "I'm still figuring this out, but here's what I've learned so far …" demonstrates a growth mindset far more powerfully than any motivational poster ever could.

And perhaps most importantly, vulnerable leaders demonstrate that they understand the emotional impact of change on their team, and actively support those who may be struggling - a key aspect during large-scale transformations.

But true vulnerability isn't just about words; it requires a shift in how you lead.

> **?** How comfortable are you with vulnerability as a leader? Do you openly admit when you've changed your mind, or struggled to find a solution?

Walking the Walk: Modeling Adaptability

Change leaders don't just preach adaptability; they live it every day by, for example, embracing the ambiguity that comes with overhauling systems and processes throughout the transformation journey.

During transformation, you need leaders who can reframe challenges not as failures but as opportunities to refine the implementation plan. These leaders must visibly demonstrate a commitment to continuous learning, recognizing that transformation will never follow a linear path.

Linking back to the power of vulnerability, your change leaders should resist the urge to provide a quick, but ill-conceived answer, just for the sake of appearing decisive. Instead, they must model comfort with "*not knowing yet*," seeking input from their team and gathering more data before deciding.

Remember that unexpected roadblocks aren't always derailments, and your leaders need to be skilled in asking questions like:

> **?** What assumptions did we have about stakeholder buy-in that turned out to be incorrect?
> How might we need to adjust our communication strategy to address this?

Finally, since transformations often necessitate workforce reskilling and upskilling, your leaders must visibly embrace growth. They can seek out new technology tools, attend cross-functional workshops, or even temporarily join a different team.

Remember: Walking the walk is contagious! Your leaders' passion for learning will inspire their teams to step outside their comfort zones and embrace growth as an essential part of the transformation process.

Painting a Compelling Vision

> **?** Have you ever launched a strategic initiative, only to see misalignment across departments hinder its potential?

Organizational transformations mean supplying employees with more than just a list of planned changes. You must demonstrate a compelling vision of why the changes are necessary and how they will create a better future for both the organization and its people.

Your leaders must also be master storytellers, crafting a narrative that illustrates what success looks like in a way that's both emotionally resonant and achievable. Leaders must actively help employees connect their daily tasks to your ultimate "North Star" vision. This will demonstrate how even seemingly small contributions can have a significant impact on reaching the goal.

Keep in mind that for your transformation to succeed, it's critical to have change leaders who consistently highlight progress and recognize those working toward the vision. This will help maintain momentum and motivation throughout the often-lengthy transformation process.

Driving the Change

Imagine a leader who is comfortable with the status quo, never questioning or challenging established practices.

> **?** Could such a leader truly inspire the bold actions required for transformative success?

Change leaders cannot afford to be just passengers on the transformation journey - they actively define and steer the course of the transformation. This role requires them not to be afraid of challenging the status quo, asking difficult questions, and pushing for better solutions, even when it causes temporary discomfort.

Their influence extends beyond mere task execution.

They must view their role as one of streamlining bureaucracy while proactively identifying and removing obstacles that, while not directly related to strategic initiatives, may impede the overall progress of the transformation. To truly inspire enthusiasm and commitment across the team, they must also possess a genuine passion for the transformation's potential.

The "And More" Factor

While vulnerability, adaptability, vision, and a drive for change are crucial during transformation, it's important to remember that these qualities don't replace traditional leadership skills, including:

- Making strategic decisions based on data and sound judgment.
- Allocating resources in ways that align with transformation goals.
- Managing complex stakeholder relationships effectively.

During transformation, however, the ability to inspire, adapt, and maintain a clear focus on the vision becomes even more critical for success.

Quick Tips: Techniques for Assessing Leaders' Comfort with Vulnerability, Adaptability, Vision, and Change Action

- *Observation.* Observe how your leaders naturally behave and communicate during the transformation process. Look for specific actions demonstrating the key qualities:
  - *Vulnerability:* They openly discuss setbacks with the team, reframing them as learning opportunities.
  - *Adaptability:* They hold "lessons learned" meetings after milestones, focus on adjusting the plan, not assigning blame.
  - *Vision:* They regularly connect day-to-day tasks back to the broader goal, celebrate even small wins as progress.
  - *Change Action:* They challenge the status quo by regularly asking if there is a better way to do things, even when they are working.
- *Scenario-Based Questions:* Present leaders with hypothetical challenges they might face during the transformation. Their answers will reveal their thought process and natural leadership style.
  - *"If early data indicates the current change plan is unlikely to succeed, what actions would you take?"*
  - *"You see a potential opportunity to accelerate progress, but it requires taking temporary resources from another team. How do you approach this?"*
- *Past Successes and Failures:* Analyze past projects to identify patterns in your leader's behavior.
  - Did their solutions tend to be reactive, or did they demonstrate forward-thinking to improve processes in the long-term?
  - Did they prioritize results over employee motivation and onboarding, or find a balance between the two?

Assembling Your Change Management Team

Think about a time when you've spearheaded a project involving people from different departments.

> **?** Did miscommunication slow things down? Were essential perspectives missing during the planning stages, leading to issues later on?

Transformations are inherently complex, with the need for collaboration increasing exponentially to their scale. That's why a strong, cross-functional change management team is a crucial supporting pillar that must be continuously present throughout your transformation journey.

Leaders, unable to be present everywhere at once, can greatly benefit from a well-coordinated team that serves as their eyes and ears. This team provides vital, real-time insights from across the organization. They help to bridge gaps and smooth out challenges throughout the transformation process.

Moreover, involving employees from various departments through this team not only minimizes oversights but also fosters a more inclusive approach to change. As we discussed in previous chapters, when employees feel actively involved in shaping the transformation, they are more likely to support and champion the initiatives, reducing resistance and enhancing overall engagement.

The strategic assembly of the change management team ensures that all angles are considered, making the transformation journey more cohesive and supported every step of the way.

Whom to Include

The right Change Management team brings diverse perspectives, catches issues early, and creates buy-in within the organization. Those benefits are gained by involving the right set of people, including:

- *Project Management*: Keeps initiatives on track, coordinates team activities.

- *Human Resources (HR)*: Designs training, addresses employee concerns, plays a key role in change communication.

- *Frontline Employees*: Their on-the-ground experience identifies practical implementation issues early on.

- *Information Technology (IT)*: Ensures the technology chosen aligns with the transformation goals and anticipates potential integration challenges with existing systems.

- *Highly Impacted Departments*: Include deep expertise in the area where the change will have the biggest impact (e.g., in overhauling sales processes, a sales team representation is crucial).

Keep in mind that, like other aspects of your transformation journey, building this team is an ongoing process. As your transformation evolves, you may need to adjust its composition to align with the focus of your initiatives at that time, constantly ensuring a team that is large enough to ensure diverse representation, yet small enough to remain agile and avoid decision-making gridlock.

Quick Tips: Empower Your Change Management Team!

Assembling the right team is just the beginning. For them to truly drive the transformation, they need your support and trust. Here are some tips on how to empower them for success:

- *Autonomy*: Don't micromanage. Set clear goals and expectations, then allow the team to manage day-to-day challenges within those boundaries. Your team will grow to own their responsibilities while innovatively problem-solving their way through them.
- *Growth Opportunities*: Your change management team must have easy access to the training, mentorship, and tools

required for their maximum effectiveness. Go beyond fulfilling the requirements of their role on the change team, but also consider their overall professional development needs and wants.

- *Visibility and Recognition*: Notice and acknowledge your change team's contributions during meetings and internal communications. Encouragement and praise motivate them to go the extra mile.

Together We Transform

True change leadership isn't about maintaining the status quo - it's about unlocking the potential within your organization and its people. It requires boldness, humility, and a strong belief in the future you are creating together.

However, this is not enough. You need to invest in a culture of communication that emphasizes two-way dialogue, fostering a sense of shared purpose and collective responsibility for the transformation. With this in place, and with honest feedback and diverse perspectives flowing freely, your organization will become an engine of innovation and adaptability, ready to overcome any obstacle.

Key Takeaways

- *Change Leadership Is Not Just Management*: It requires a distinct set of skills focused on embracing uncertainty, inspiring teams, and communicating the vision.
- *Vulnerability Is a Strength*: Leaders who admit mistakes and embrace learning build trust and foster a growth-oriented culture.
- *Adaptability Is Essential*: Change leaders see challenges as opportunities, proactively seeking out new approaches and information.
- *Vision Drives Success*: Employees need to see how their work contributes to the bigger picture to stay motivated during long transformations.

- *Action-Oriented Leaders Are Key*: Change leaders aren't afraid to challenge the status quo and push for progress, even when it's uncomfortable.
- *A Cross-Functional Change Management Team Amplifies Impact*: They provide diverse perspectives, catch issues early, and build buy-in.
- *Empowering the Team Is Crucial*: Giving the team autonomy and supporting their growth fosters ownership and innovation.

Case Study: FINxP PAYMENTS - A FINTECH TRANSFORMATION JOURNEY (Continued)

(The company's name has been changed to protect its identity.)

With an ambitious roadmap for FINxP's transformation in place, the next challenge was rallying our workforce and creating a culture that embraced change.

We knew that successful transformation required more than just a well-articulated plan, especially since FINxP Payments had enjoyed past success. To achieve the "North Star" vision we had defined, a fundamental mindset shift was needed.

FINxP required a willingness to embrace new ways of working along with leadership that modeled the desired behaviors. It was clear that several employees were still clinging to the "old way" of doing things, and that needed to change. However, before focusing on the cultural issue first, we wanted to ensure that there is clear vision how we intended to achieve our "North Star" as the destination, though highly interesting, sounded very challenging at face value.

Planning for Transformation Success

To achieve our ambitious "North Star," the first step was to break the vision down into a detailed, actionable plan that built upon the strategic initiatives we'd identified earlier on. This involved:

- *Gap Analysis*: We conducted a deep dive into our current state, identifying specific pain points in our processes, technology, and capabilities. This helped us prioritize initiatives and allocate resources effectively. For example, we realized that our legacy systems were not only hindering scalability but also impacting our ability to offer personalized customer experiences.

- *Prioritizing for Impact*: Each initiative was carefully evaluated based on its impact on our "North Star," its feasibility considering resources, and the risks it brought. This analysis helped identify the most critical areas of focus.

- *Aligning Resources with Goals*: We developed a plan that allowed for comprehensive resource allocation based on the prioritized initiatives. This catered for new technology budgets, training, and external partnerships. The plan also identified internal resources that could be reallocated or repurposed to support the transformation.

- *Measuring Progress*: Clear, measurable goals and key performance indicators were developed to track progress and maintain accountability. This, later, allowed our team to identify early wins, celebrate successes, and make data-driven adjustments as needed.

Building a Culture of Change

With a solid plan in place, we turned our attention to the heart of transformation: our people. A transition toward a culture that embraced change was necessary. Such a change meant fostering a growth mindset, encouraging continuous learning, and establishing adaptability as a pillar for the organization.

The growth mindset was introduced through interactive workshops and training sessions. Apart from explaining the theory behind fixed versus growth mindsets, these sessions provided employees with practical tools and techniques for identifying their own beliefs and actively shifting toward a more adaptable and resilient perspective.

Building on this foundation, we went beyond theory and created a psychologically safe environment where experimentation and risk-taking were encouraged. We understood that a fear of failure was a major obstacle to innovation. To address this, we implemented several initiatives:

- *Failure Forums*: By establishing these forums, employees could openly share stories of their "noble failures." These were projects that did not go as planned yet yielded valuable lessons. The forums helped normalize the concept of failure as a learning opportunity rather than a career ending mistake.

- *"No Blame" Policy*: The company formalized its value of learning over perfection by explicitly communicating and practicing it. Honest mistakes made in pursuit of innovation would not be punished.

- *Effort Recognition*: Instead of focusing solely on outcomes, we started recognizing and rewarding employees for their efforts to learn, experiment, and take calculated risks. The recognition exemplified that the journey toward innovation was just as important as the destination.

Leading The Change

FINxP's cultural shift could not have been achieved without the pivotal role of its leaders. Executives became change champions who modeled the desired behaviors and actively communicated the "why" behind the transformation.

They participated in training programs, openly discussed their own learning journeys, and actively sought feedback from employees. Their efforts created an atmosphere of transparency and collaboration.

Furthermore, leaders regularly reinforced the "North Star" vision, connecting it to individual roles and team goals. They used storytelling to make the vision relatable and inspiring, highlighting the positive impact of the transformation on both employees and customers. We also identified and empowered change champions at all levels of the organization, further amplifying our message and ensuring that the change was embraced throughout the company.

By harmonizing our culture, leadership, and planning efforts, we created a unified and collaborative environment where everyone was moving toward the same goals. This had set the stage for the next phase of our transformation journey, where communication, adaptability, and employee empowerment would become our greatest assets.

Explore Further

Ancillary questions and supporting materials related to this case study are available to help you apply the concepts introduced in this stage. These resources can be accessed through the QR code provided in the Preface section.

STAGE 3

Integrate

CHAPTER 7

Communication as the Engine of Change

"Communication is the real work of leadership."

—Nitin Nohria

Introduction: Building Connections Through Communication

Communication plays a critical and essential role in your organization's transformation alongside the key leadership qualities required for a successful change.

Communicating effectively involves more than simply transmitting a message. Within their audience, communicators must foster understanding, build trust, and inspire collective action. Their skills must serve as a bridge that connects visionary leadership with tangible results, ensuring that transformations are not merely implemented, but embraced as a shared journey by the entire organization.

Yet, despite recognizing its importance, many leaders struggle with communication during times of change. Ask yourself:

> Are you primarily focused on getting your point across to your employees, or are you actively listening to their concerns and ideas?
>
> Are you able to paint a picture of your organization's "to-be" state that resonates with people both logically and emotionally?
>
> Is your communication style adaptive to the audience you are addressing? Are you able to make sure everyone feels heard and understood?

Listening as the Foundation of Communication

Effective communication during transformation is a two-way street. It starts with truly listening. That means noticing not just the words spoken, but the underlying emotions, concerns, and aspirations of your employees.

Think of a time when you felt truly heard.

> **?** Were you able to change your perspective?
> Were you more willing to support the person who had truly listened to you?

Putting in a conscious effort to understand the complete message being conveyed includes noticing nonverbal cues and underlying emotions. It involves asking clarifying questions, paraphrasing what you've heard, and showing empathy for the speaker's perspective.

Through active listening, you can:

- *Build Trust*: Employees who feel heard implicitly trust their leaders more. This means they are more ready to embrace the changes required for your transformation.

- *Drive Better Decision Making*: Feedback and insights from various levels within your organization mean more informed and effective decisions. Through active listening, leaders can catch issues early, adapt their strategies in real time and align themselves better with the organization's needs.

- *Uncover Hidden Issues*: Resistance to change may often be a symptom of unspoken fears or reservations. By actively listening, you can uncover these issues and address them proactively.

- *Create Buy-In*: Employees who feel their concerns are taken seriously are more likely to become advocates for the transformation. As a result, your transformation goals will have a wider reach without additional effort.

Quick Tips: Practical Tips for Active Listening

Quick Tips

- *Focus*: Ensure you are fully present in the conversation by eliminating distractions.
- *Open-Ended Questions*: Ask questions that allow speakers to elaborate on their point. Use "what," "how," or "tell me more about ..." questions to seek out detailed responses.
- *Reflect Back*: Speakers will feel heard and understood if you are able to paraphrase their concerns, issues, or ideas in a succinct and accurate way.
- *Nonverbal Cues*: Communication involves more than speech. Notice both your and your speaker's body language and tone of voice.

Identifying and Prioritizing Key Stakeholders

Apart from communicating effectively with your employees, it's crucial to remember that they are not a monolithic entity. Your staff comprise a diverse group of individuals and teams with varying levels of influence, interest, and stakes in the outcome.

Who Are Your Stakeholders?

Before prioritizing your stakeholders, take a moment to brainstorm the diverse individuals and groups involved, both directly and indirectly, in your organization's transformation.

Your stakeholder list should go beyond the decision makers. Keep an eye for influencers and those whose work will be directly impacted, including internal stakeholders such as employees and managers, and external ones like customers, partners, investors, and regulators.

By widening the spectrum of stakeholders considered, your communication and engagement strategies can be tailored better.

Prioritizing Your Stakeholder Engagement

During periods of change, time is a precious commodity, particularly in the early stages of transformation. While, ideally, you reach out to each and every identified stakeholder, the sad reality is that you may not manage to. Consequently, you will need to optimize your time by prioritizing your communication efforts based on several factors, including:

Power and Influence

Identify stakeholders who can sway decisions or significantly impact the transformation journey. Engaging with these individuals early on is crucial to secure their support and leverage their influence to positively affect others.

Level of Impact

Prioritize those who will be directly and significantly impacted by the change. Also, be cautious of those who might be less impacted but could still cause you larger issues, perhaps because of their network within your organization.

Interest

Some stakeholders may have a genuine interest in your transformation. Keeping these individuals engaged can be invaluable, as their positive word of mouth can serve as powerful marketing for your change initiatives.

Proximity to Transformation

Give priority to the people who will be impacted first. Their experiences and opinions will set the tone for others, shaping perceptions of the change. Failing to onboard these stakeholders early could lead your changes to feel forced and their expertise ignored, making your journey more difficult.

By strategically prioritizing your stakeholders based on these factors, you'll ensure your communication efforts are targeted, effective, and build the buy-in necessary for a successful transformation.

Adapting Your Message for Different Audiences

Think of your company as a symphony orchestra, with each section playing a different instrument. To achieve harmony, the conductor must tailor their communication to each section's unique needs and perspectives.

In the same way, different stakeholders within your organization may require particular or targeted communication styles to ensure your messages' effectiveness. Avoid adopting a one-size fits all approach to your communication. Instead, build your communication with intention, adjusting the language, level of detail, and channels to best suit each group.

Also keep in mind that different audiences will have particular interests and concerns. For example, while executives might prioritize financial results and strategic alignment, frontline employees may focus on how the changes will impact their daily work. This makes it crucial to tailor your message based on the audiences' interests and concerns to keep them engaged.

Furthermore, consider your audience's technical background. Ensure your language is clear and accessible by avoiding jargon with those outside the project team.

Taking the time to understand and adapt your messaging to your audience's unique needs is not just a "nice to have." It's a critical success factor that builds trust, empowers employees, and lays the groundwork for the entire organization to embrace the changes ahead.

Quick Tips: Communication Strategies for Different Stakeholders

Quick Tips

- *Leadership*: Focus on vision, strategy, and transparency, conveying the rationale, benefits, costs, and risks associated with the transformation. Provide regular, concise updates, avoiding lengthy emails and presentations.
- *Employees*: Strive for inclusivity by seeking feedback, addressing concerns, and celebrating successes together. Town halls, open forums, and surveys are effective tools. Use clear language, avoid jargon, and articulate the reasons for the transformation and expected changes. Show employees the benefits they will gain while being transparent about challenges and the potential need for upskilling. Remember, communication should be two-way and therefore, you need to establish channels for feedback, questions, and suggestions.
- *Customers:* Proactively inform customers about upcoming changes, explaining why they are necessary and highlighting the benefits they can expect. Clearly communicate potential disruptions, along with mitigation plans, to build trust. Create dedicated channels for customer queries and concerns,

ensuring a responsive support team that can address issues promptly. Finally, keep customers informed about the progress of their issues and the overall transformation journey through regular updates to demonstrate your commitment to transparency.

- *Suppliers:* Engage suppliers early on to maintain a seamless supply chain by, for example, establishing digital platforms (shared databases, online portals, collaborative software) for efficient communication and information exchange. Provide clear guidelines regarding changes in processes, timelines, and expectations. Schedule regular meetings with key suppliers to facilitate open communication and address concerns.

- *Regulatory Bodies:* Provide regular updates to regulatory bodies, communicating clearly and proactively about changes in processes or practices to ensure alignment with regulatory requirements. Assign dedicated personnel to act as liaisons for prompt resolution of compliance-related queries. Conduct periodic audits to assess and proactively address potential issues while demonstrating transparency and commitment to regulatory adherence.

- *Community:* Organize forums where community members can voice opinions, concerns, and suggestions. Publish reports highlighting the transformation's positive impact on social responsibility. Actively participate in community events and initiatives to demonstrate a hands-on approach and to gather feedback in real time.

Leaders as Communication Champions

The leadership qualities discussed in the previous chapter - vulnerability, adaptability, a compelling vision, and the drive for change - are significantly enhanced when used alongside effective communication.

As you lead your transformation, remember that communication goes beyond just sending emails and newsletters or holding occasional town halls. It's a continuous, intentional process that demands a comprehensive approach where your leadership team must take on several important roles:

- *Active Listeners*: By genuinely listening to the concerns and feedback of their teams, leaders show that they value their opinions, building trust during times of uncertainty.

- *Transparent Communicators*: Open communication creates a sense of shared purpose and encourages collaboration. Leaders who are honest about challenges and celebrate successes create a culture of trust and accountability.

- *Storytellers*: Clearly showing how the transformation will positively impact both the people and the organization they form part of will inspire and motivate employees.

- *Data-Driven Evaluators*: Leaders must consistently measure the effectiveness of their communication efforts by gathering feedback through surveys, focus groups, or informal conversations. Such feedback will allow communicators to tailor their messages to truly connect with stakeholders.

By taking on these key roles, your leadership team will both create a shared understanding of the transformation vision and empower employees to actively participate in the change process. These factors will ultimately drive your organization toward a successful and sustainable future.

From Conversation to Collaboration

Your organization's entire change process hinges on having effective communication that can go beyond being a checkbox-ticking exercise. By actively listening to your employees, adapting your message for diverse stakeholders, and proactively addressing communication barriers, you're not just transmitting information - you're building trust, fostering collaboration, and creating a shared sense of purpose.

Successful transformations are built on a foundation of open dialogue. As your organization evolves, so too must your communication strategies. Remaining adaptable and committed to continuous feedback, will ensure that your message not only resonates but also inspires action.

While technology can enhance communication during transformations, remember that at its heart, transformation is about people, their ideas, and their willingness to embrace change. However,

> **?** Are your employees equipped with the skills needed to embrace and implement the changes you envision?

Key Takeaways

- *Communication Is Key*: Successful transformation requires effective communication. This goes beyond information transfer, additionally building trust, fostering collaboration, and creating a shared vision.
- *Active Listening Builds Trust*: Times of change require leaders to build trust by actively listening to their employees with respect and empathy.
- *Tailored Communication*: Your communication style should adapt to your audience and stakeholders, ensuring everyone understands and embraces the transformation.
- *Leadership as Champions*: Leaders who model transparency, active listening, and storytelling skills create a culture of open communication that drives change.
- *Data-Driven Evaluation*: Regularly measure the impact of your communication efforts to ensure your message resonates effectively with all stakeholders.
- *People are Central*: While technology can enhance communication, the heart of transformation lies in engaging employees. Understand their needs and empower them to participate actively in the change process.

CHAPTER 8

Fostering an Adaptable Workforce

"The illiterate of the 21st century will not be those who cannot read and write, but those who cannot learn, unlearn, and relearn."

—Alvin Toffler

Introduction: Your People, Your Future

The previous chapter looked at how effective communication can inspire and align your team throughout a transformation. Nevertheless, even the most well-articulated vision and communication strategies fail if your organization is not capable of adapting to the unforeseen challenges each transformation will bring about.

Consider an orchestra conductor. While they may be able to stir an orchestra with a vision for musical excellence, if its musicians are not able to adapt to the complexities of a new symphony, their performance will fall flat.

Transformations work in the same way. Constantly evolving technology, fluctuating global markets, and uncertain economic conditions mean that an agile, adaptable organizational culture is not just beneficial but crucial for your organization's survival.

From Training Events to Learning Journeys

Transformations often require you to reskill and upskill your existing workforce to meet new demands. As we saw earlier, a thorough gap analysis will reveal whether your team's capabilities align with your "To-Be" vision and how to identify room for growth.

Since transformations are continuous and cyclic, filling this gap means more than just implementing training programs. A cultural shift toward continuous learning and development fosters adaptability and empowers your employees to evolve alongside your organization.

The Limitations of Traditional Training

Think back to the last mandatory training session you attended.

> **?** Did it truly ignite a passion for learning within you? Or was it uninspiring and quickly forgotten once you returned to your daily tasks?

Traditional training programs often fall short because they are isolated and episodic events aimed at teaching specific skills for a singular context. While valuable in some situations, this approach does not nurture the continuous growth and adaptability your organization needs to thrive in a changing landscape.

Embracing Continuous Learning

Conversely, a continuous learning culture works like a well-maintained engine that can constantly achieve its peak performance. The change is in the mindset, from one focused on one-time events to one that prioritizes the ongoing processes of skill development, knowledge acquisition, and personal growth. This approach has numerous benefits including:

- *Increased Employee Engagement*: When learning becomes a regular part of work, employees feel valued through investments into their professional development. Increased engagement means higher productivity, creativity, and a willingness to embrace change.

- *Greater Agility and Adaptability*: Employees who embrace constant learning can better handle unforeseen challenges, pivoting strategies when needed. Experimenting, learning from mistakes, and developing new skills become second nature.

- *Enhanced Innovation*: Curiosity, creativity, and a willingness to explore new ideas all serve as fuel for the proactive innovation that differentiates top organizations from competitors.

Quick Tips: Creating a Culture of Continuous Learning

Quick Tips

- *Leaders as Role Models*: Your organization's leaders must actively promote and participate in learning initiatives. Their involvement sends a powerful message to the entire organization.
- *Learning in Daily Work*: Within your organization, learning should exist as an integral part of daily work rather than a once-in-a-while activity. Learning and experimentation periods should be commonplace within your employees' workday or week.
- *Personalized Learning Paths*: By tailoring learning experiences to the needs and career goals of individual employees, personal and professional growth goals are better achieved. These experiences could involve a mix of online courses, workshops, and seminars.
- *Leverage Technology*: Utilize technology to provide learning options that are more easily accessible. Online learning platforms can range from formalized courses to microlearning modules that employees can complete at their own pace.
- *Foster a Safe Environment for Failure*: The workplace should be an environment where employees feel safe to experiment and fail in their work. Innovation and improvement are expedited when embracing failure as part of the learning process.
- *Encourage Knowledge Sharing*: Regular knowledge-sharing sessions allow employees to share their experiences. These can include best practices, personal or external case studies, and lessons learned, enhancing collective growth and building a sense of community.
- *Recognition and Rewards*: Developmental and learning efforts should be consistently recognized and rewarded. Formal recognition programs, promotions, and acknowledgment during team meetings boost morale and motivation.

Knowledge Sharing as a Core Skill

While a learning-oriented culture is crucial, individual learning is only one piece of the puzzle for successful transformation.

Think of a sports team where each player refuses to pass the ball - each player might be impressive individually, but their global performance will suffer without teamwork.

Similarly, this can happen within your organization. If knowledge becomes trapped within individuals or departments, collaboration is limited, impeding progress toward your transformation goals. This underscores the necessity for you and your leadership team to actively foster a knowledge-sharing culture.

Pause for a moment and reflect:

> **?** Does your current organizational culture encourage knowledge hoarding?
> Do you see examples of information being held tightly by individuals or teams, instead of being shared for the greater good?

A way to break down these silos is to encourage people from different departments to work together on specific tasks. Envision software engineers working alongside customer service representatives, or a marketing expert collaborating with a finance analyst. A cross-pollination of ideas leads to the engineer gaining a deeper understanding of customer pain points and the representative learning about technical possibilities. Together, they create more innovative solutions.

While technology can also play a vital role in facilitating this shift - through implementing knowledge management systems, collaboration platforms, or online forums where employees can easily share ideas and ask questions - the same techniques used for individual upskilling and reskilling can be used to successfully transition to this mindset shift. This includes incentivizing, rewarding, and publicly recognizing those who actively contribute to the knowledge-sharing culture.

Remember that by recognizing knowledge sharing, you foster collaboration and innovation within a resilient workforce that is better equipped to handle the complexities and challenges that will arise during your transformation journey.

Measuring Adaptability

While it is crucial to foster a culture of continuous learning and knowledge sharing, it's essential to evaluate how these efforts are translating into actual adaptability within your workforce.

> **?** Are your initiatives genuinely equipping your employees to handle new challenges and embrace change effectively?

Traditional performance reviews, while important, often focus on past achievements and individual output, such as sales figures or project completion rates. These measures fall short in capturing the flexibility and growth mindset that your transformation truly requires.

Gauging your organization's readiness for change, goes beyond using traditional metrics to assess the ability to learn, adapt, and innovate. For such intangible yet essential qualities, consider using the following key indicators to assess your workforce:

- *Learning Agility*: This is the speed at which your employees learn new skills and adapt to unfamiliar situations.
  Are new concepts quickly grasped and applied to your employees' work?

- *Problem-Solving Skills:* The ways in which employees tackle problems requiring both individual and collaborative solutions reveals much about attitudes toward challenges.
  Are creativity, resourcefulness, and a "can-do" attitude present when obstacles arise?

- *Openness to Feedback*: Regularly ask for and provide feedback from and to your team. Individuals' responses allow you to assess

whether a growth mindset is present for both positive and con-
structive input.

Do they actively seek feedback, reflect on it, and incorporate it
into their work?

- *Willingness To Experiment*: Observe whether employees take
initiative, experiment with novel ideas, and actively seek out
challenges.

  Do your employees embrace new approaches, even if it means
venturing outside their comfort zones?

- *Collaboration And Communication:* Assess your employees' level of
communication and collaboration in different instances.

  Do you see people actively seeking out collaboration opportunities, communicating their ideas clearly, and being receptive to the
perspectives of others?

These approaches broaden your evaluation criteria away from just traditional metrics. They include organizational adaptability, helping you gain
a more comprehensive view of your organization's readiness to face future
challenges and opportunities.

Such targeted assessment helps identify areas needing improvement.
Efforts can then be focused on the areas in which they are most needed,
ultimately driving your organization to become more agile and innovative
in overcoming transformation challenges.

Adaptability as Your Competitive Edge

Transformations hold only one certainty: *change*. By proactively building
a workforce capable of rapid learning and adaptation, not only do you
prepare your organization for change, but you ensure a competitive advantage over those who resist deviation from the status quo.

The paths to transformation are rarely smooth. Resistance to change
is a natural human response, stemming from a mix of emotions like fear,
uncertainty, and anxiety from a loss of control.

But remember, resistance isn't a sign of failure but rather an opportunity to listen, learn, and adapt your approach accordingly.

Key Takeaways

- *Continuous Learning Is Key*: Fostering a culture of continuous learning and knowledge sharing is essential for building an adaptable workforce capable of taking the dynamic environment brought about by your transformation head-on.
- *Move Beyond Traditional Training*: Shift away from one-time training events and embrace continuous learning that prioritizes personalized development plans, mentorship, and collaboration.
- *Break Down Silos*: Encourage collaboration and knowledge sharing across teams to leverage collective intelligence and foster innovation.
- *Measure Adaptability Holistically*: Go beyond traditional performance metrics and assess qualities like learning agility, problem-solving skills, openness to feedback, willingness to experiment, and collaboration to gauge your organization's readiness for change.
- *Empower Your Employees*: Create a safe space for experimentation, encourage risk-taking, and recognize learning efforts to encourage a growth mindset and promote adaptability within your workforce.

CHAPTER 9

Turning Resistance Into Resilience

When it comes to change, the most difficult thing is to let go of what we know and believe."

—Charles F. Glassman

Introduction: The Resistance Barrier

When leaders say, "Our employees are resistant to change," an image of hard-headed and flawed employees is painted. Ask yourself: *Is that attitude consistent with reality?*

Change can be unsettling, but it's important to understand that resistance isn't necessarily a sign of defiance or stubbornness. More often, it's a symptom of deeper issues: fear of the unknown or improper communication, whether stemming from lack of information or a feeling of not being heard. Left unaddressed, resistance can fester, hindering your transformation's progress as negativity propagates throughout the organization.

But here's the good news: There are ways to reduce or even overcome resistance. By understanding its root causes and employing proactive strategies, you can transform resistance into a promoter for change.

Instead of a roadblock, it can become an opportunity to build trust, strengthen collaboration, and empower your employees to actively contribute to the transformation journey.

Beyond "They Just Don't Get It"

It's easy to think of those resisting change as simply "not getting it." Instead of jumping to oversimplified conclusions, think:

> **?** Have you ever stopped to ask yourself why they're not getting?

Imagine trying to drive a car with a flat tire - simply telling the tire it "doesn't get it" won't solve the problem. You need to find the puncture and repair it.

Similarly, leaders must dig deeper into the various forms of resistance to find effective solutions. First, they must understand the different ways resistance can present itself. These may include:

- *Active Resistance*: This is the easiest form to identify as active re-sisters openly express their opposition to the change. This could include engaging in debates, voicing negative opinions, or influencing others to push back against the initiatives.

- *Passive Resistance*: This subtler form involves behaviors such as procrastination, silence, minimal compliance, or carrying work out to mediocre standards. Those who resist change passively may agree to it outwardly while concurrently dragging their feet or not fully engaging with the new changes.

- *Passive-Aggressive Resistance*: This form of resistance combines elements of both passive and aggressive resistance. Look out for employees who ostensibly support the changes but then sabo-tage and undermine efforts to carry them out. This could mean rumors being spread, misinforming peers about the changes, or failing to provide the support needed for the change to succeed.

A one-size-fits-all solution that addresses resistance to change is impossi-ble. This is because the ways in which people resist change depend highly on their personal traits and why they are resisting it. Place importance on understanding the reasons behind such resistance by considering the following possible root causes:

Fear of the Unknown

Many employees resist change simply because they don't know what it entails. Therefore, resistance might stem from the paralyzing uncertainty that comes from a lack of clear communication on what the changes involve and how they would impact employees.

Discomfort with Change

Disrupted routines may lead even the most skilled employees to feel incompetent. The discomfort may lead to resistance as employees struggle to adapt to new ways of working.

Job Security

Changes in organizational structure or technology can lead employees to worry about job redundancies. The fear of job loss is a powerful motivator for resistance. If employees perceive threats to their livelihoods, they may resist as a means of self-preservation.

Lack of Perceived Benefits

If planned changes are not perceived as beneficial, employees may be quick to question their value. Highlight both organizational and individual upsides to paint compelling pictures of your proposed "to-be" state.

Lack of Trust

If the organization has a history of broken promises or poor communication from leadership, employees may lack faith in the transformation's goals or methods.

To effectively manage and mitigate resistance, leaders must go beyond simply recognizing these factors and actively engage with their teams. Instead, they need to work hard to create an environment where open communication is encouraged, and feedback is sought and respected. However,

> **?** Are you and your leaders prepared to listen empathetically and respond honestly to concerns with concrete information and support?

Quick Tips

Quick Tips: Strategies for Addressing Resistance

- *Empathy First:* Start by understanding the emotional root of resistance. Active listening is key here.

- *Transparency and Communication*: Share as much information as possible about the change. Explain the "why" and "how," along with the anticipated timeline. Be clear about what's still unknown and what decisions are still being made.
- *Involve Employees in the Process*: People who feel valued are more likely to buy into your ideas. Involve them in problem-solving, get their input on implementation details, and create opportunities for feedback.
- *Focus on Small Wins*: Early successes create momentum and show the tangible benefits of the change. Reinforce the positive impact by celebrating the wins publicly.
- *Address Skills Gaps*: If you identify a lack of skills or knowledge as the root of the resistance, provide targeted training in the form of personalized learning journeys and make sure to support employees to feel confident in their new roles.

Change Champions as Allies

While you and your leadership team are crucial in mitigating resistance, the reality is that you can't be everywhere at once. Even if you could, employees are generally more open to listening, hearing, and believing messages from people with whom they have built relationships and trust, rather than from a leadership team with whom they don't have a close relationship. This is where "change champions" become invaluable.

Change champions are influential individuals across your organization, chosen for their passion and ability to inspire their peers. They don't necessarily hold formal authority, but their informal influence is crucial for driving the cultural adoption of change. They work at the grassroots level, translating the vision into relatable terms, addressing fears, and demonstrating the benefits of change through their own actions.

Consider this example: A hospital undergoing a digital transformation might have a nurse who's passionate about technology. She becomes a change champion, not only demonstrating the new tools but also easing their colleagues' anxieties by guiding them through the system. This type of grassroots influence will lead to faster adoption and greater buy-in than top-down directives alone.

One of the best things about change champions is that they act as your organization's "word-of-mouth" marketing for the transformation. Their networks extend the reach of your message beyond the core team, helping it resonate in departments where it might otherwise be met with skepticism. Furthermore, they offer you on-the-ground insights, helping you to proactively identify potential roadblocks and finding solutions.

Finally, through the Change Champions, you are bridging the gap between official communication and day-to-day reality, making the change feel less like a directive from senior management but more like a shared journey.

Quick Tips

Quick Tips: Identifying and Empowering Your Change Champions

- *Look for Passion and Influence*: Which persons from your organization demonstrate the most enthusiasm for your planned changes? Do they have a reputation for getting things done?
- *Empower Them*: Once identified, supply those persons with the tools and resources they need to become advocates for the transformation. Provide early access to technology, communications training, or opportunities to share their experiences.
- *Recognize Their Contributions*: Make sure their efforts are publicly acknowledged and rewarded, reinforcing their organizational value and inspiring others to follow their lead.

Early Wins as Persuasion

Now that you've understood the ways in which resistance to change originates and presents itself, and how to identify key influencers, you've laid down the groundwork for change. Despite this, keep in mind that transformations are more like a marathon than a sprint.

? How do you maintain energy and enthusiasm, especially when faced with the setbacks that arise during any major change initiative?

As a response to uncertainty, people seek tangible evidence that the changes you're implementing are having a positive impact. So, naturally, the answer to this key question lies in prioritizing and celebrating early wins.

Think of these as small, tangible victories that demonstrate the transformation is not just a theoretical concept, but a reality already taking shape. These early wins can be as simple as a streamlined process that saves employees time, or a new tool that improves efficiency. Their common benefit is that they are noticeable enough to demonstrate progress and keep momentum.

When employees see the benefits of change firsthand, they become more receptive to future initiatives. By choosing the right quick wins, you are, therefore, setting the stage for sustained engagement and enthusiasm throughout your entire transformation journey.

Quick Tips: Choosing the Right Quick Wins

- *Visibility and Impact*: Choose initiatives whose impacts are easily noticeable by employees, customers, or key stakeholders. By maximizing the number of people experiencing the benefits, you grow their momentum.
- *Empower through Feasibility and Speed*: Prioritize initiatives that can be implemented quickly and with minimal disruption to daily operations. The goal is to demonstrate progress in a timely manner.
- *Alignment with Goals*: Quick wins should closely align with your "North Star" vision, serving as microcosms of your long-term goals. Ignore initiatives that are easy but don't contribute to the overall transformation strategy.

When Resistance Isn't the Real Issue

We've spent much of this chapter exploring the psychology behind resistance to change and the ways it can be mitigated. What should be your next move if, despite your best efforts to listen and empathize, resistance persists?

In some cases, what appears to be resistance might be a symptom of deeper, systemic issues within your organization. These underlying problems can be harder to spot, as they often masquerade as simple pushback against change.

For instance, imagine a team resisting a new workflow. The surface reason might be "we're too busy to learn something new." But upon deeper investigation, you may discover that the underlying issue is a lack of resources or an unrealistic deadline, creating an environment where the team feels set up for failure. Other issues might be confusing processes, unclear roles and responsibilities, or even a lack of trust in the person leading the change.

This makes it crucial not to assume that resistance is always a psychological issue caused by people clinging to the status quo. Instead, adopt a detective's mindset. Listen deeply to your team's concerns, look for patterns in their feedback, and involve your change champions to uncover the root causes of resistance.

By proactively addressing these underlying issues, you not only overcome resistance but also build a stronger, more resilient organization that is well equipped to successfully navigate the entire transformation journey.

Key Takeaways

- *The Many Faces of Resistance*: Change can be resisted actively, passively, or passive-aggressively. Identifying which of these issues you're facing means addressing them more effectively.
- *Uncover the Root Causes*: Deeper issues, such as fear of the unknown, job insecurity, discomfort with change, imperceptible benefits, or a lack of trust could all contribute to change resistance.
- *Engage Change Champions*: Identify influential and change-passionate individuals within your organization and transform them into advocates for your vision to build support among peers.
- *Prioritize Early Wins*: Focus on achieving small, tangible victories early in the transformation journey. "Quick wins" help build momentum, boost morale, and demonstrate the value of change.

- *Foster Open Communication and Collaboration*: Your organization should champion open dialogue, active listening, and employee involvement to build trust and encourage buy-in for your vision.
- *Adapt to the Unexpected*: Be prepared to adjust your transformation strategies and initiatives based on feedback, emerging challenges, and the evolving needs of your organization.
- *Address Underlying Issues*: Don't mistake systemic issues like resource deficiencies or confusing processes for psychologically rooted resistance to change. By identifying and addressing the root causes, you can create a more adaptable and resilient organization.

Case Study: FINxP PAYMENTS - A FINTECH TRANSFORMATION JOURNEY (Continued)

(The company's name has been changed to protect its identity.)

With a solid plan in place and a change-ready culture taking root, the next phase of our transformation was to ensure that all the elements were seamlessly integrated into the daily workings of FINxP Payments. This required a concerted effort to prioritize continuous and effective communication, adaptability, and proactive resistance management - the key ingredients for making the change stick.

Communication as the Engine of Change

Communicating our transformation ahead of its execution needed to be done effectively with leaders and frontline employees alike. A multi-pronged approach was adopted:

- *Listening as a Communication Tool*: Since communication is a two-way street, we launched surveys, focus groups, and one-on-one conversation sessions with employees to garner insights. This allowed messaging to be refined and for concerns to be proactively addressed.

- *Adapting Our Message*: Different people have different needs. Communicating the changes meant using messages tailored to each audience. For executives, we used data-driven presentations, while with frontline employees, more story-driven communication was employed.

- *Leadership as Champions*: Our leaders took on the change by communicating it themselves and modeling the desired behaviors. Their example created a sense of shared purpose and empowered employees to become champions of the change themselves.

- *Overcoming Communication Barriers*: We took note of the potential obstacles to our communications, such as information overload, a lack of trust, and language barriers. We tackled such issues by using short, jargon-free messaging, while ensuring that trusted and well-skilled communicators were chosen depending on the audience and subject discussed.

Promoting an Adaptable Workforce

To truly empower our team and create an adaptable workforce that embraces transformation, we knew we had to go beyond traditional, one-size-fits-all training methods. Our vision for the company was for an organization that had a vibrant learning culture, with employees who felt valued, supported, and equipped to grow.

In order to achieve this, a personalized learning journey was created for each employee, given the uniqueness of each person's career goals and existing skills. These tailored learning paths included a mix of online courses, job shadowing opportunities, and targeted workshops - addressing both the technical and the soft skills required. As a result of the learning-oriented changes, employees were more engaged and eager to take ownership of their own professional growth.

Furthermore, to accelerate learning and encourage experimentation, we created a "sandbox" environment where teams could safely test new technologies and processes before they were fully implemented. This hands-on approach sped up the learning curve and fostered a sense of ownership and excitement for the change.

To break down the silos that plagued FINxP Payments' existing operations, an internal knowledge-sharing platform was launched. This allowed employees to share best practices, seek colleagues' advice while also celebrating each other's successes. The online hub quickly became a vibrant driver for innovation, sparking conversations and generating new ideas for the change.

Additionally, we implemented a robust mentorship program, pairing experienced employees with those transitioning to new roles or needing additional support. In this way, knowledge could be more easily transferred through a safe learning space that allowed for questions and learning from past experiences, ultimately building confidence in new roles.

We didn't just focus on technical skills. We also recognized the importance of developing an agile mindset. We incorporated Agile methodologies into our training programs, emphasizing the value of iterative learning, continuous feedback, and embracing change as a constant.

Turning Resistance Into Resilience

Despite our efforts to build a change-ready culture, the inevitable resistance was something we wanted to be prepared for. So, we proactively identified and addressed it through:

- *Understanding the Root Causes*: We dug deeper than surface-level complaints to understand the underlying fears and concerns driving employee resistance.

- *Empowering Change Champions*: We leveraged the influence of specific employees, turning them into change champions to address concerns, share information, and build enthusiasm for the transformation.

- *Prioritizing Early Wins*: We focused on achieving quick wins and highlighting successes, demonstrating the benefits of the change and creating positive momentum.

The Impact

These efforts bore fruit quickly. Employees developed new skills while concurrently embraced a more proactive, solutions-oriented approach. For example, a design thinking workshop spurred our customer service team to implement a new complaints tracking system, significantly improving response times and boosting customer satisfaction.

This, together with the investment in building a collaborative and adaptable spirit across the whole organization, meant a profound cultural shift that was fundamental to FINxP's growth in the ever-evolving fintech landscape.

Explore Further

Ancillary questions and supporting materials related to this case study are available to help you apply the concepts introduced in this stage. These resources can be accessed through the QR code provided in the Preface section.

STAGE 4

Facilitate

CHAPTER 10

Innovation as a Core Driver

"Innovation is taking two things that already exist and putting them together in a new way."

—**Tom Freston**

Introduction: The Power of Innovation

Imagine two competing companies facing the same market disruption. One company chooses not to react, instead bidding its time by clinging to outdated practices. Its competitor recognizes the opportunity presented by the disruption, adapting their products and services to quickly meet the new customer demands.

> **?** Which company is more likely to become the market leader, rather than just survive?

This scenario demonstrates how innovation is a core driver of an organization's success, rather than simply a nice-to-have factor during times of transformation.

Innovation Isn't Just About the "Next Big Thing"

Innovative organizations go far beyond simply creating new products or services. Instead, it is a mindset that allows companies to approach challenges and opportunities with creativity, curiosity, and an openness to calculated risks.

But why is it such a crucial driver for your transformation journey?

Simply put, companies that fail to innovate quickly become irrelevant, exemplified by Kodak in earlier chapters, who struggled to adapt to shifting customer needs and behaviors.

Innovation doesn't just impact the bottom line but instead carries additional effects throughout your entire organization.

Employees are drawn to workplaces that promote creativity and offer opportunities to contribute to meaningful change. This means that a work culture that prioritizes innovation can itself breed it by attracting and retaining top talent.

Exemplifying this, Google adopted a "20 percent time" policy that allows employees to dedicate a portion of their working hours toward personal projects. The ideas gleaned from exploring other projects can then feed back into more innovative solutions to Google's own goals, boosting morale and creativity.

Innovation also serves as a powerful tool for enhanced customer satisfaction. By anticipating changing customer needs, brand reputation and customer loyalty are strengthened. A great example of this is Amazon's consistent approach toward improving customer experiences, leading to a higher customer satisfaction that subsequently drives loyalty.

Innovation Is Much More Than Just Technology

Technological breakthroughs, while deeply impactful, represent just a single facet of innovation. Transformations are truly driven when innovation is seen as a comprehensive company strategy that touches upon various organizational aspects.

Think of innovation as the engine of your transformation vehicle - an engine that requires multiple cylinders firing in harmony to operate efficiently. Similarly, there are many ways to innovate within your organization, each playing a key role to a successful transformation.

Here's how to tap into diverse innovation avenues within your organization:

- *Customer Segmentation*: Evaluate whom you serve. Are there new customer segments you could target or existing ones with unmet needs you could better address?

- *Product/Service Offerings*: Consider your offerings. Could you expand your product or service line, bundle offerings differently, or create entirely new value propositions?

- *Revenue Models*: Reflect on your revenue generation strategies. Could alternative models like subscriptions, freemium services, or dynamic pricing unlock new growth avenues?

- *Delivery and Distribution Channels*: Analyze how you deliver value. Could leveraging new channels, forming strategic partnerships, or employing advanced technologies enhance your reach and effectiveness?

By examining these questions, you'll gain a clearer understanding of how innovation can drive your transformation forward. As you reflect on these, ask yourself:

> **?** Where are the hidden opportunities for innovation within my organization, and how can we activate the potential for innovation within our organization to achieve the "North Star" vision?

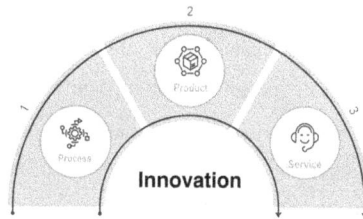

Figure 6: The Innovation Landscape

Product Innovation: The Reinvention of What You Offer

True innovation to your products and services means moving beyond just minor tweaks and superficial updates. Instead, you must create or transform your offerings into ones that will truly resonate with customers - thus putting your customers truly at the center of your operations. This means not only developing products that address their pain points, but also introducing elements within your product suite that exceed their expectations.

For example, ahead of the iPhone's introduction in 2007, smartphones existed as relatively clunky and business-oriented devices. Apple's innovation meant they were reimagined into devices that could seamlessly blend communication, entertainment, and productivity into a user-friendly package. Similarly, Nintendo's introduction of the Wii video game console meant the medium was suddenly open to a wider markets and demographics. While other gaming companies had catered to hardcore gamers, Nintendo's Wii targeted families and casual players - new markets that drove sales.

Product innovation is often the most visible aspect of a transformation, both for your customers and employees. Besides driving growth and enhancing customer satisfaction, innovation also sparks internal motivation as employees their contributions produce tangible impacts.

However, remember, product innovation is a continuous process. Your organization's offerings must be continuously adapted to meet evolving customer needs and market demands.

Quick Tips: Strategies for Fostering Product Innovation

Quick Tips

- *Invest in Research and Development*: Dedicate a portion of your organization's resources into exploring new technologies, analyzing marketing trends, and identifying unmet customer needs.
- *Create a Culture of Creativity*: Encourage employees to experiment and take risks in pursuit of innovation. Brainstorming sessions, hackathons, and idea-generation programs can be implemented to include contributions from employees at all levels.
- *Listen to Your Customers*: Gather feedback through surveys, focus groups, and social media monitoring to understand what your customers want and need.

Process Innovation: Streamlining for Speed and Efficiency

Besides innovation that breeds new products and services, think about the ways your organization does things:

How long does it take to get a new product to market?

How many steps are involved in onboarding a new client?

Do your employees spend more time fighting outdated systems than actually doing their jobs?

Is the answer to any of these questions "too long," or "too many"? If so, it's time to take a closer look at your processes.

While a new product release is an exciting, highly visible and tangible innovation, it is the streamlined and efficient processes that truly fuel your business' growth. They are the backbone of how your organization operates - without them, your company cannot deliver its products or services to its customers.

Inefficiencies in your company's processes mean increased costs and wasted time. These issues could then lead to frustrated employees, dissatisfied customers, and even disaster if left to fester in the long run.

Process innovation is not just about reducing the steps involved. Instead, it looks at eliminating bottlenecks, identifying redundancies, and optimizing how work gets done at each of those steps.

Imagine a health care provider struggling with long patient wait times. By taking a look at their appointment scheduling process, they might discover that delays are caused by manual data entry and a lack of coordination between departments. Rather than eliminating the steps involves, one needs to focus on strategically streamlining and reworking the processes to maximize value. In doing so, patient satisfaction, loyalty, and health care outcomes could be drastically improved.

This internal efficiency would lay the groundwork for delivering exceptional customer service, a key stepping stone toward achieving the "North Star" vision.

💡 Quick Tips: Strategies for Driving Process Innovation

Quick Tips

- *Process Mapping:* Create a visual map that outlines your current processes. This will help identify bottlenecks, redundancies, and areas ripe for innovation. This could be done through a simple flowchart, value stream map, or swimlane diagram.
- *Data Analysis:* Obtain data showing your processes' cycle times and error rates. Alongside customer feedback, this can help you identify areas of underperformance. Such a data-driven approach helps pinpoint the root causes of inefficiencies while prioritizing improvement efforts.

- *Employee Involvement*: Your frontline employees may often have the knowledge and expertise your managerial perspective is missing. Tap into these valuable insights to streamline work-flows and improve processes.
- *Embrace Technology*: Assess how new technologies can innova-tive on your current processes. This could include automation tools, artificial intelligence, or digitization's that streamline tasks and free up employees for more human-driven work.
- *Continuous Improvement*: Settling for a one-time fix is not an option for your organization. Instead, aim for continuous innovation of the ways in which your companies work by involving employee input.

Service Innovation: Enhancing the Customer Experience

While product and process innovations may inspire a customer's first purchase, service innovations turn them into loyal advocates for your brand.

In line with your customer-centric approach, consider your com-pany's contact points. Are clients being transferred aimlessly between departments when reaching out? Alternatively, are they immediately con-nected to knowledgeable representatives who can offer tailored solutions and advice?

Keep in mind that each interaction with your organization, from the initial inquiry to post-purchase support, should be designed to exceed customer expectations. Achieving this is no easy feat, requiring innova-tive thinking and a commitment to continuous improvement from your organization.

Quick Tips

Quick Tips: Strategies for Driving Service Innovation

- *Map Customer Journeys*: Think of a customer's potential con-tact points with your organization. Whether it's website visits, phone calls, or in-person interactions with representatives, each avenue should be analyzed for potential pain points and improvement opportunities.

- *Invest in Customer Service Training*: Aside from technical knowledge, your employees should be equipped with the necessary soft skills for delivering exception service. This means empathy, active listening, problem-solving, and communication.
- *Empower Frontline Employees*: Your customer-facing staff should be able to take decisions for the customer's benefit. Without this autonomy, they cannot resolve issues quickly and their creativity is hampered.
- *Leverage Technology*: Customer interactions can be streamlined through tools such as chatbots, self-service portals, and CRM (customer relationship management) systems. These should provide quick access to information, personalize the experience and minimize frustration.
- *Gather and Act on Feedback*: Do not ignore feedback gathered from surveys, focus groups, and social media. Use it to identify areas for improvement and introduce changes that address the issues.

Embedding Innovation in Your DNA

Innovative organizations are not defined by luck or short-lived trends. Instead, they are ones who prioritize longer-lived qualities in the way they approach their changing environment, including their capabilities to adapt to economic shifts, market dynamics, competition, and shifts in customer behavior.

However, this change in approach requires more than just individual passion. Leaders must consciously act in unison toward building a supportive work environment that embraces creativity and experimentation for enhanced innovation. The key question is:

? Are you ready for this innovative ecosystem in your own organization?

Key Takeaways

- *Innovation Is Essential*: Beyond simply creating new products or services, innovation should be seen as a mindset that enables organizations to adapt, thrive, and lead.
- *A Multifaceted Approach*: Products, processes, and services can all benefit from innovation, whether it impacts your organization's marketing, revenue model, or structure.
- *Customer-Centricity Drives Innovation*: Customer needs and feedback should drive and uncover areas requiring innovation. Understand and anticipate by considering the client's point of view.
- *Innovation Requires More Than Technology*: While technology can be an enabler, promoting a culture of creativity, risk-taking, and collaboration is essential for sustaining innovation.
- *Continuous Improvement is Key*: Innovation is an ongoing journey. By constantly seeking out new ideas and refining existing ones, you ensure your organization remains adaptable and competitive.

CHAPTER 11

Fostering an Innovation Ecosystem

Alone we can do so little; together we can do so much."

—Hellen Keller

Introduction: Building Your Ecosystem

Now that we've established why innovation is a core driver for success in your organizational transformation, it's time to explore how it can be implemented. From words to action, what changes can your organization introduce to grow the creative, risk-taking, and knowledge-hungry workforce required for growth and client satisfaction?

Besides the individual mindset shift we've covered, your organization must adopt a strategy for an idea-nurturing environment ready to develop, test, and integrate its core operations.

Creating a Safe Space for Innovation

Innovation is inherently messy. It involves trial and error, false starts, and even outright failures. Compare it to the scientific method: While experiments may not always yield the expected results, they invariably provide valuable insights.

All of this requires you to build an ecosystem where this messy process is acknowledged and valued, where the board of directors and C-level executives support you in investing in innovation, and where your employees aren't afraid of a "failed" experiment.

This means investing in the right leadership, a supportive organizational structure, adequate resources, rewards for innovation, and a data-driven decision-making culture.

But remember, a safe space for innovation doesn't mean a free-for-all. Instead of wild suppositions, calculated risks should be encouraged, replacing the fear of failure with a desire for learning and growth.

Leadership: Setting the Tone

Leadership plays a pivotal role in fostering innovation within your organization. Leaders who embrace vulnerability, adaptability, and a compelling vision set a powerful example.

Their commitment to your transformation must go beyond words. Leaders should contribute toward to creation of an innovative environment by:

- *Encouraging Risk-Taking*: Taking calculated risks shouldn't just be encouraged by the team handling the transformative process. Instead, leaders across the organization must adopt the new mindset, taking decisions that confirm failures are not career-ending mistakes.

- *Celebrating Failures*: Crucially, leaders must emphasize that valuable insights can be gleamed from each failure, normalizing it as an essential step in the learning process.

- *Empowering Employees*: Implement initiatives such as "innovation sprints" that allow team members to take ownership of their ideas while providing the tools and autonomy required to explore and implement them.

When leaders invest in their team's creative potential, both financially and with their time, they send a clear message: *Innovation isn't just valued, it's expected.*

Structure: Building for Agility

> **?** Is innovation supported or hindered by your current organizational structure?

An organization's structure - its hierarchies, communication, and culture - influence the way its individual employees think and act. Because of this, rigid echelons, complicated pecking orders, and siloed departments can all be innovation killers.

Your transformation should rethink traditional models for structuring organizations and find ways to create a more agile framework that promotes innovation.

Flatter organizational hierarchies are one way to empower more employees at all levels to make decisions. This means shorter chains between ultimate decision makers and frontline employees. Such systems break down silos by establishing teams that are cross-functional and able to tackle complex challengers from diverse perspectives.

Decentralized decision making presents another option for rethinking an organization's structure. It allows independent teams to act quickly and decisively based on their understanding of customer needs and market trends.

Adopting agile methodologies that promote iterative work cycles and continuous feedback can further enhance your organization's ability for innovation.

Resources: Investing in Innovation

Innovation is only possible when the required financial resources and time are dedicated and available. Your organization should allocate a portion of its budget specifically for innovation initiatives. These could include funding for prototyping, testing, and implementing new ideas, alongside investments into workforce training and upskilling.

> **?** Have you allocated a specific budget for innovation initiatives? What percentage of your overall budget does it represent? Are there areas where you could increase investment to foster a more innovative culture?

Creating dedicated spaces for innovation, such as innovation labs or hackathons, can also ignite creativity and collaboration. Encourage teams to set aside time each week or month to brainstorm, experiment, and explore new ideas. Don't hesitate to look outside your organization for support. External experts, start-ups, or universities can provide valuable resources and a fresh perspective on challenges.

Rewards and Recognition: Celebrating the Changemakers

Apart from the intrinsic value of recognizing and rewarding innovative behaviors, recognition can serve as a strategic way to foster an innovative culture within your organization. It sends a clear message that shows that your organization values creativity, risk-taking, and idea generation.

Employees whose contributions are seen, celebrated, and rewarded are more likely to experiment further, pushing boundaries and driving transformative change. Consider implementing the following strategies to build an innovation system within your own organization:

- *Innovation Awards*: An awards program that recognizes and celebrates your workforce's best innovation efforts will go a long way to solidify morale and an innovation culture. Reward innovative products, process improvements, and customer experience upgrades through company events, internal newsletters, or your organization's intranet.

- *Financial Incentives*: Boost your workforce's intrinsic motivation with financial incentives. This could mean bonuses or profit-sharing agreements in return for successful innovation projects. These perks should be dependent on measurable outcomes like increased revenue, improved efficiency, or enhanced customer satisfaction.

- *Career Advancement Opportunities*: Offer career advancement opportunities to individuals who demonstrate a passion for innovation and a drive for improvement. Promotions and leadership roles within innovation teams or special projects will allow them to further develop their skills.

- *"Idea Bounties"*: Incentivize employees to submit ideas for your organization's improvement by involving prizes or bounties for successful implementations. Through a spirit of healthy competition, creativity and workforce contribution can be increased.

- *Informal Recognition*: Go beyond systemic forms of recognition by genuinely reaching out to passionate employees through simple acts. Whether a handwritten thank-you note, a shout-out during team meetings or a gift card, these small gestures go a long way to show appreciation.

Data: The Fuel for Innovation

Innovation is intrinsically linked with data. The upcoming final stage of the SHIFT framework explores the full power data can deliver to your organization. For now, it's enough to know that only by collecting and analyzing data you can have a meaningful understanding of your customers' behavior, market trends, and internal processes.

Such insights can help you identify opportunities for improvement or else validate new ideas. Once your organization embraces data-driven decision making, it will become better at identifying risks, and predicting outcomes for truly driven innovation to happen.

Quick Tips: Tips for Building Your Innovation Engine

Quick Tips

- *Empower the "Intrapreneurs"*: Identify employees who exhibit passion and the entrepreneurial spirit. Trust them to lead small-scale projects, even if they seem unrelated to their primary roles. This builds a sense of ownership and cultivates a risk-taking.
- *Celebrate the "Noble Failures"*: Some innovative initiatives will not go as planned. Rather than killing morale by assigning blame, focus on the lessons that can be gleamed. A "Lessons Learned Wall" at your offices, open to contributions from anyone, will make insights visible and create a share knowledge base for future efforts.
- *Make Time for Ideation*: Don't just talk about innovation; schedule dedicated time for it. Block off an hour each week for brainstorming sessions, idea pitches, or even individual reflection time. This demonstrates your commitment and gives innovation the priority it deserves.

- *Data Democratization*: Don't let data be siloed within specific departments. Provide access to relevant data and offer training in basic analysis tools to employees across the organization. This empowers them to use data to inform their ideas and track their own progress.

Building a Community of Innovators

While stereotypical depictions of innovation may involve sole thinkers leading the charge ahead of colleagues, the true power of innovation is only unlocked collaboratively. Even the most brilliant and independent minds benefit from diverse perspectives and a shared knowledge base.

Open-source software development communities such as GitHub provide the perfect example, hosting countless developers who contribute their expertise to create robust, thoroughly scrutinized, and innovative solutions. This collaborative approach stands as a testament to the power of collective problem-solving.

By providing a similar community within your organization, like-minded individuals, both within and outside your company, can exchange ideas, tackle challenges, and celebrate successes. Such a collective intelligence accelerates solutions development and fosters a share sense of purpose, serving as the fuel for your transformation journey.

When individuals are connected to a larger pool of innovators, they are motivated and supported to produce their own efforts. This powerful sense of community drives engagement, raising productivity, creativity, and the willingness to take risks.

By fostering a strong innovation community, you create a self-sustaining engine for continuous improvement and transformation.

Quick Tips: Strategies for Building an Innovation Community

- *Internal Social Networks*: Create accessible Internet-based spaces where employees can connect, share ideas, discuss challenges, and celebrate success. This could be a bespoke companywide social network, a Slack channel, or a forum dedicated to innovative thinking.

- *Mentorship Programs*: Pair experienced innovators with newer employees or those with less experience. Such partnerships build skills and accelerate the learning curve.
- *Innovation Challenges and Hackathons*: Such events create a diverse melting pot of individuals to brainstorm solutions to specific problems or explore opportunities. They can serve as the impetus for fostering creativity and camaraderie, thereby leading to breakthrough ideas.
- *Industry Events and Conferences*: Employees who are given the opportunity to attend these events could network with industry peers, learn about the latest trends, and gain inspiration from competing innovators.
- *External Partnerships*: Open your organization to collaborations with universities, research institutions, think tanks, or other companies in your industry. Such partnerships mean interaction with new perspectives, technologies, and talent.

Monitoring and Adapting the Ecosystem

Once a safe space for innovation has been invested in and created, alongside a fostered culture of continuous learning, transformation leaders must step back and assess progress.

> Have your efforts led to changes? Are there true improvements? Are employees actively engaged in the innovation process?
> Have you seen tangible results, such as new ideas being implemented or improved customer satisfaction?

Answering these questions means gaining a critical perspective on just how effective your innovation ecosystem is.

Just as you analyzed your organization's readiness for change in the previous chapters, you now need to apply that same data-driven approach to your innovation ecosystem. This means establishing clear metrics and goals to track progress.

This could take the form of measuring the number of new ideas generated, the percentage then implemented, or the impact on customer satisfaction scores.

Alongside such insights, regularly collected and analyzed data from surveys, employees and your innovation platforms will allow for a holistic view of what works and what doesn't. This builds the insight and confidence to adapt your approaches accordingly, continuously driving your organization toward its "North Star."

Key Takeaways

- *Innovation Is a Holistic Endeavor*: Aside from individual creativity and passion, innovation ecosystems require a supportive and inclusive environment that incubates ideas from every level of the organization.
- *Leadership Sets the Tone*: Only when innovation is championed firsthand by leaders and failures embraced as learning opportunities are employees empowered to experiment and develop their own ideas.
- *Structure Matters*: Rigid and hierarchical organizational structures exert a chokehold on innovation. Flat power chains, cross-functional collaboration, decentralized decision making and agile approaches create more adaptable and innovative environments.
- *Resources Are Essential*: Without the proper investments in time, budget, and tools, innovation will be hard-pressed to flourish. Create dedicated spaces and allocate resources for experimentation to foster a culture of innovation.
- *Data Fuels Innovation*: Gain valuable insights, identify opportunities, and validate ideas by collecting and analyzing data on customer behavior, market trends, and internal processes.
- *Rewards and Recognition Drive Engagement*: By celebrating and rewarding innovative behavior, you create positive feedback loops that encourage continuous improvement and attract talent.

- *Community Is Key*: Accelerate innovation and drive your transformation by fostering a sense of community for your innovators' ideas to be encouraged and for collaboration to grow.
- *Monitor and Adapt*: Regularly evaluate the effectiveness of your initiatives, collect feedback, and be willing to adapt your approach to ensure continued success.

CHAPTER 12

Experimentation and Learning Loops

"Innovation is not just about ideas. It's about making ideas happen."
—Scott Belsky

Introduction: The Power of Experimentation

> **?** Have you ever been hesitant to act on a promising idea because you haven't yet figured out its perfect solution?

The importance and potential of innovation can only be realized through experimentation - the critical mechanism that brings it to life. Despite how essential it is for driving transformations, many organizations fear experimentation, discarding it as a frivolous waste of time and resources.

Let's be honest - those concerns are valid. After all, failed experiments/ projects can be costly and damaging to morale.

When conducted strategically, experiments are not akin to throwing ideas at the wall to see what sticks. Instead, they create a controlled environment, a physical or virtual "lab" where teams can test, learn, and adapt their approaches before committing to full-scale implementation.

Think of these experiments as pilot programs for your new initiatives, allowing you to gain crucial data that power informed decisions while minimizing risk.

Why Experimentation Is Crucial for Transformation

Experimentation serves as the bridge between innovative ideas and real-world results. Just as scientists test hypotheses to gain knowledge, organizations must experiment to:

- *Validate Assumptions*: Try out ideas in controlled environments to boost confidence in their potential impact.

- *Reduce Risk*: Limit the risk of potentially unsuccessful ideas by experimenting on a smaller scale before making costly or irreversible commitments.

- *Accelerate Learning*: Adopting the "fail fast, learn fast" mentality that comes with experimentation means accelerated learning opportunities for your leaders and workforce

- *Foster a Culture of Innovation*: Experimentation allows employees to take calculated risks, fosters collaboration, and teaches through mistakes. It also presents employees with avenues to contribute their ideas and perspectives.

- *Drive Data-Driven Decision Making*: Data gathered from both failed and successful experimentation means informed and more confident decision making on strategy adjustments, initiative prioritization, and closer alignment with your "North Star" vision.

By embracing experimentation as a core part of your transformation journey, you're not just taking a chance; you're investing in a systematic approach that reduces risk, accelerates learning, and, ultimately, drives innovation.

Designing Effective Experiments

A detective is trying to solve a murder mystery. Does he aimlessly gather clues in the hope of stumbling across the answer?

No. Instead, there is a hypothesis - a theory about what happened - with evidence systematically gathered proving or disproving it.

In the same way, a clear and solid hypothesis is at the core of effective experimentation - a clear and testable statement that attempts to predict the impact of specific changes during your transformations.

Crafting Your Hypothesis

Whether you're building a new feature for increased customer engagement, streamlining processes, or testing the effectiveness of a new marketing strategy, you should clearly define the problem you are trying to solve. This helps keep any experimentation relevant and targeted.

Next, form a clear prediction of what you expect to happen after the idea is implemented. Will there be increased sales? Improved efficiency? Higher employee satisfaction?

Finally, identify your key variables: the ingredients that shape the impact of your changes. The factors you intend to change are your independent variables. Those you will measure to determine the impact of your changes serve as the dependent variables. This clarity is crucial for interpreting the results accurately.

An example, hypothesis for changes to improve customer satisfaction might be: "By implementing a new chatbot on our support portal, we'll reduce customer wait times by 50 percent and increase customer satisfaction scores by 10 percent."

The outcome of our dependent variables, the wait times and satisfaction, relies on our independent variable, the new chatbot.

Experiment Design Essentials

Following your definition of a clear hypothesis, you must design the experiment itself. Make your experiments more effective by striving to minimize biases and maximizing the reliability and validity of the results.

This often means using distinct control and experimental groups to isolate the impact of your changes. The participants comprising your groups should be divided randomly. Where possible, also obscure their group assignment to avoid exerting influence on the results.

Implementing the Experiment

Several types of experiments can be conducted:

1. *A/B Testing*: Comparing two versions of a product, website, or marketing campaign.
2. *Pilot Programs*: Small-scale implementations of a new idea before a full rollout.
3. *Controlled Experiments*: Using a control group and an experimental group to isolate the impact of a specific variable.

Choosing the right methodology depends on the specific hypothesis, resources, and desired rigor of your experiment.

The results of your first tests may surprise you, but you must keep in mind that experiments are iterative. Analyze data, learn from mistakes, and refine the approach for your next round of testing.

By embracing a culture of experimentation, you can accelerate your transformation journey through continuous improvement and innovation.

Quick Tips

Quick Tips: Making the Most of A/B Testing

- *Define a Clear Hypothesis and Success Metrics Before Starting*: Be specific. An example hypothesis could posit that changing the color of a call-to-action button will increase click-through rates. Also specify the measurable metrics, whether click-through rates, conversion rates, or time on page.
- *Ensure a Statistically Significant Sample Size*: Experiments with a larger participant base are more indicative of actual effects. Use sample size calculators or the help of a statistician to make sure you exceed the minimum sample size for meaningful conclusions.
- *Test Only One Variable at a Time*: Making changes to multiple factors will prevent you from confidently attributing effects to specific changes. Focus on one element, whether a headline, image, or button color, while keeping all else consistent.

- *Utilize User-Friendly A/B Testing Tools*: A/B testing can be simplified through tools like Optimizely, VWO, and Google Optimize. These platforms automatically create variations, split web traffic, and collect data for your experiment. Focus on analysis and decisions by saving time and resources.
- *Be Patient and Allow for Sufficient Testing Time*: Refrain from skipping to conclusions and allow your experiment enough time to yield significant results. This could mean testing for weeks or months, depending on web traffic or user base.

Rapid Prototyping: Accelerating Innovation

Real transformations depend on bringing brilliant ideas to life.

Rapid prototyping involves quick and cost-effective testing without commitment to full-scale implementation. Given transformations thrive on agility and speed, this approach is particularly crucial.

Why Rapid Prototyping Matters

When leading your organization's transformation, you must recognize the importance of adopting a rapid prototyping approach. Wielded as a tool, it allows for your assumptions to be quickly tested, thus revealing potential flaws and gathering valuable insights before resources are sunk.

A planned rapid prototyping phase for your project will furnish you with the insights to take properly informed decisions. This knowledge can validate ideas and concurrently reduce the risk of costly errors or setbacks, guiding the successful implementation of your transformation.

Integrating Prototyping into Your Transformation Strategy

Keep in mind that rapid prototyping shouldn't be an isolated activity. To maximize its value, it needs to be intentionally integrated into your broader innovation strategy. This means aligning prototype development with your North Star vision and the strategic goals you defined earlier in this transformation journey.

The rapid prototyping phase similarly involves active collaboration across teams and functions. Your organizational readiness assessment can once again be used to determine the areas in which prototyping is most likely embraced, and where it could expose weaknesses or opportunities.

Say that analyses and assessments of your organization's current state revealed a lack of customer-centricity. The rapid prototyping of a new customer service process could provide invaluable feedback on whether the introduction of this new process will help improve matters, or if more fundamental changes are required to help you achieve your objectives.

Rapid prototyping thrives in environments that enable open communication and shared ownership. By encouraging risk-taking and transparency around the prototyping process, you can boost the learning-centric culture we discussed in earlier chapters.

Types of Prototypes

Since prototyping is a cyclical process, the idea or project being worked on will exist in distinct phases, including:

1. *Basic Prototype*: This is the most basic form of your idea. Often, this means a simple sketch or mock-up that serves as a starting point for concept exploration and initial feedback.
2. *Functional Prototype*: At this stage, your idea is developed enough to simulate how it will function in the real world. This allows for more in-depth testing and evaluation.
3. *Presentation Prototype*: Here, your idea is polished enough to be showcased to stakeholders. While perhaps lacking final touches, this prototype should clearly demonstrate key features and benefits.

The prototypes you need to create will depend highly on your goals, resources, and the stage at which your project exists. Early on, basic prototypes may be sufficient. Close to implementation, functional or presentation prototypes shine.

This rapid prototyping concept in conjunction with the "fail fast, learn fast" mentality is the perfect ingredient to guiding you transform your ideas into successful innovations throughout your transformation journey.

> ### 💡 Quick Tips: Building Blocks for Your Rapid Prototyping Approach
> **Quick Tips**
>
> - *Concept Sketching*: Your initial sketches should outline key features and functionalities, serving as quick visual representations.
> - *3D Models*: Using CAD software or similar tools, develop more detailed 3D models. While intangible, these precise models can help you assess your product's design better.
> - *Prototype Creation*: Take advantage of rapid prototyping tools such as 3D printing or software simulation for quick testing and evaluation of a physical or digital prototype.
> - *User Testing*: Engage real users to test the prototype. Collect comprehensive feedback on usability, design, functionality, and other critical aspects.
> - *Iteration*: Refine the prototype based on the feedback received. Make necessary adjustments and repeat the testing phase as needed. Each iteration should aim to bring the product closer to market.

A Short Note About Data: The Engine Behind Experimentation

Without adequate data, all of your experimentation is reduced to mere guesswork. Collect as much information about your project as possible while it is being developed and prototyped for easy referencing and informed iterations.

The data you collect will serve as the evidence that ultimately validates or disproves your hypothesis, measures progress, and allows for informed prioritization of initiatives. Without it, your transformation is deprived of a compass and map for its journey.

Data isn't just about numbers and spreadsheets. It's about gathering insights into customer behavior, operational efficiency, and the overall impact of your transformation efforts. It's about using those insights to iterate, adapt, and optimize your approach.

We'll dive deeper into how to build a data-driven transformation at a later stage in this book. For now, remember that every experiment you conduct should be designed to generate data you can learn from. This evidence-based approach is what allows you to make informed decisions and continuously improve your innovation efforts.

Key Takeaways

- *Experimentation Fuels Innovation*: It allows your approach to be tested, learned from, and adapted to bridge the gap between ideas and full implementation.
- *Hypotheses Guide Experiments*: Your problem should be clearly defined alongside with informed predictions and key variables to measure, ensuring your experiments are focused and data driven.
- *Experiment Design Is Crucial*: Effective design, including control groups, randomization, and blinding, helps minimize bias and increase the reliability of results.
- *Rapid Prototyping Saves Time and Money*: By building quick, low-cost prototypes you can validate assumptions, identify flaws, and gather feedback early.
- *Data Drives Learning*: Make sure to collect ample data from your experimentation and prototyping for easy referencing, informed decision making, and continuous improvement.
- *Innovation Requires Diverse Perspectives*: By involving input from across your organization, more aspects of your problem are considered, helping you collect key insights through different perspectives.

Case Study: FINxP PAYMENTS - A FINTECH TRANSFORMATION JOURNEY (Continued)

(The company's name has been changed to protect its identity.)

With a unified, engaged workforce and a culture that embraced change, we had the perfect conditions to transition FINxP Payments into a more innovative organization. This would facilitate our efforts to achieve our ambitious vision of becoming the Global Operating System for Small Business E-commerce.

Innovation as a Core Driver

We began by asking employees what "innovation" meant to them. Unsurprisingly, most responses focused on technology and new products. However, to truly achieve our vision, we needed to be innovative in all areas of the business - our processes, services, and even how we approached customer interactions.

To broaden this understanding, we encouraged everyone - from frontline employees to senior leaders - to embrace curiosity and question assumptions in everything they did. We hosted "Innovation Fridays," where employees could pitch any idea, regardless of their department or role.

The initiative's success was in how widely it was implemented, opening an avenue for innovative ideas to more than just the "techies." This established that innovation was something everyone could contribute to.

Fostering an Innovation Ecosystem

While "Innovation Fridays" generated a wealth of fresh ideas, their success hinged on them being part of an ongoing and sustainable process. An innovation ecosystem was needed - a vibrant culture that encouraged collaboration and creativity for ideas to be developed and implemented properly.

Our leadership team led the charge. Their hands-on and active approach served as a model for the rest of the company, making it clear that taking risks was encouraged, and that even failed experiments were valuable learning opportunities. This meant active participation in brainstorming sessions and hackathons while concurrently, a portion of the annual budget was dedicated to innovation initiatives.

These changes provided the motivation, funding, and resources for the prototyping, testing, and implementation of promising ideas. By de-prioritizing short-term profits, the leaders signaled innovation was a top priority.

To reduce stifling effects on creativity, FINxP Payments' hierarchical structure was flattened through cross-functional teams with real decision-making power. Previously siloed departments were opened up through new communication channels, allowing for a more collaborative atmosphere that sought out diversified perspectives.

The initiatives were further fueled through the launch of an "innovation lab," serving as a space for employees to tinker creatively and problem-solve away from daily routines. Data analytics that considered customer feedback, market trends, and internal performance were also collected to help identify improvement opportunities and measure impacts. Ideas could then be quickly validated through informed decisions and a strategy that adapted as needed.

Finally, we knew that recognizing and rewarding innovative behaviors was essential for building a sustainable innovation culture. We implemented an "Innovation Awards" program, celebrating both small wins and major breakthroughs. We offered financial incentives for successful projects and career advancement opportunities for those who consistently demonstrated a passion for innovation.

Experimentation and Learning Loops

Given the impossibility of each idea being a success, a "fail fast, learn fast" mentality was adopted early on. A rigorous experimentation framework that created a controlled experimentation environment with data gathering and feedback processes helped inform decisions.

For example, ahead of a new feature's launch within our cross-border payments platform, a prototype was created and tested with a small group of customers. The insights gained helped quickly identify and address usability issues before rollout.

Outcomes and Impact

Through all these efforts, we successfully launched innovative new products and services that directly addressed customer needs, leading to an expansion of our market share. Our customer satisfaction scores soared as we delivered a more seamless and personalized experience. Internally, employee engagement and retention rates increased as our workforce felt empowered to contribute to the company's success.

Our dedication to innovation paid off, proving that a change-ready culture and a willingness to take calculated risks can lead to remarkable results. Within two years of embarking on this transformation journey, FINxP Payments not only weathered the storm of increased competition but also emerged as a stronger, more agile, and innovative leader in the fintech industry.

Explore Further

Ancillary questions and supporting materials related to this case study are available to help you apply the concepts introduced in this stage. These resources can be accessed through the QR code provided in the Preface section.

STAGE 5

Transform

CHAPTER 13

Choosing the Right Change Management Frameworks

"Change is situational. Transition, on the other hand, is psychological. It's not enough to throw out the old and bring in the new. The pathway is as important as the change itself."

—**William Bridges**

Introduction: Toward a Structured Approach

In preparing for your organization's transformation journey, you've so far assessed its readiness for change, crafted a compelling "North Star" vision with a roadmap and key initiatives, and considered your resources. Additionally, you've also looked at how to foster innovation within your organization to nurture bright ideas to fruition. Looking ahead, consider the following:

> ❓ Has a never-ending to-do list ever overwhelmed you to the point of not knowing where to start?
> Have projects you've worked on lost steam and derailed because of a lack of structure, despite starting out with great enthusiasm?

Change management frameworks have been developed and proven over decades to tackle exactly these issues. By providing your changes with a backbone comprising time-tested principles and practical knowledge, they can successfully guide your transformation.

Why Frameworks Matter

To put it simply - think of your transformation as a complex maze. The maze can be tackled in multiple ways; you could wander aimlessly hoping to happen upon the exit, or you could use a map to successfully navigate it. Change management frameworks, developed by those who have successfully navigated the maze before you, are that map.

Unlike the common misconception that they stifle creativity or impose rigid rules, change management frameworks are about providing a proven structure, a set of guiding principles, and best practices gleaned from countless successful transformations.

They are, therefore, your transformation GPS, guiding you toward your "North Star."!

In fact, a well-chosen framework offers numerous benefits for your organization while going through your transformation journey, including:

- *Structured Approach*: By breaking down complex processes into manageable phases, they become less overwhelming and easier to implement.

- *Proven Principles*: Insights, principles and practices gleamed from other successful transformations help you better achieve your goals.

- *Risk Mitigation*: Such strategies help you preempt and anticipate roadblocks and pitfalls before they have the chance to derail your progress.

- *Clear Communication*: Guidance on communicating to your teams ensures clear understanding of roles and heightened motivation to contribute.

- *Measurement and Evaluation*: Metrics and tools to track progress enable data-driven decisions and course correction as needed.

The benefits of using a structured change management framework are clear. Studies show how organizations that utilize structured change management systems can achieve their transformation goals easier, equipping their teams with the tools to succeed.

Popular Change Management Frameworks

Change management frameworks are as varied as they are useful. This makes selecting the appropriate one for both your transformation and your organization an important task. While the intricacies of each framework go beyond the scope of this chapter, by highlighting the unique strengths and perspective of popular frameworks you will be better poised to look into the ones that will work best for your situation.

Kotter's Eight-Step Process

Dr John Kotter's classic model involves a linear, step-by-step approach to change. A sense of urgency is created to build a powerful guiding coalition of leaders. Vision creation, its communication and empowerment follow. Motivating short-term wins are generated with change ultimately embedded into the organization's culture.

Large organizations with hierarchical structures may find Kotter's structured and momentum-building approach particularly applicable.

Lewin's Change Model

Kurt Lewin's Change Model views change as a three-step process comprised of "unfreezing," "changing," and "refreezing" stages. As each stage's name implies, the model calls for a challenge of the organization's existing state, the implementation of new behaviors, processes, or structures, and their subsequent solidification and reinforcement.

While not as detailed as other frameworks, Lewin's model offers a simplified and clear overview of the change process, easily communicable to stakeholders.

ADKAR Model

Developed by change management firm Prosci, the ADKAR model focuses on the individual's journey through change.

Prosci breaks down the process into five key stages: Awareness, Desire, Knowledge, Ability, and Reinforcement. The framework prioritizes understanding and addressing the psychological and emotional impacts of change for individuals.

Transformations where individuals' buy-in and skill development are critical will find particular use in this framework. It guides organizations into providing the right support for their teams to succeed.

Agile Methodology

The Agile methodology is commonly associated with software development. Nevertheless, its core principles align perfectly with organizational change, boosting its potential beyond just a way of working into a powerful framework to manage change itself.

It emphasizes flexibility and continuous feedback through work in small, manageable chunks, with an adaptable plan based on feedback and results.

Agile is therefore well suited for complex transformations with evolving requirements, allowing flexibility and learning through experimentation and iteration.

The right change management framework will serve as a crucial guide for your transformation. Compare the benefits and requirements of each approach to your organization's context to select the appropriate tool that will provide the best support toward your desired future state.

But remember, no single framework is a magic bullet. You might find that combining elements from different methodologies works best for your unique needs.

Selecting the Right Framework for Your Context

Selecting the right framework is a challenging but crucial factor for success. One-size-fits-all solutions are nigh impossible to find and implement - the best frameworks are always those which align with your specific context and goals.

Given each organization has its own unique culture, structure, processes, resources, and challenges, the ideal framework for one company may not apply to another. It is important to consider several factors in your search for the right framework or a blend of frameworks.

Organizational Culture

Every organization has its own unique personality.

> **?** Is your culture hierarchical and risk-averse, where decisions flow top-down and change is often met with skepticism? Or is it more collaborative and open to new ideas, where employees are empowered to take initiative and experiment?

Answering this question is crucial as some frameworks, like Kotter's Eight-Step Process, might be better suited for hierarchical cultures, while Agile methodologies might be more effective in organizations with a strong collaborative spirit.

Size and Complexity

The scale of your organization and the complexity of your transformation will influence your framework choice.

Play to your organization's strengths: Small start-ups may be able to pivot quickly using Agile methodologies while larger enterprises may benefit from the structured guidance of Kotter's process.

> **?** How does your chosen framework address these unique factors?

Type of Change

Apart from your organization's size and complexity, the types of changes you wish to introduce will also greatly affect your choice of framework.

The simplicity of Lewin's change model might be beneficial for small, incremental changes and optimizing existing processes. Its easily understandable and straightforward approach lends itself well to such transformations.

Organizations that are looking to radically transform themselves through major overhauls to their systems, processes or business models may find more comprehensive approaches like Kotter's necessary.

While assessing your options, consider the kinds of change you would like to make:

> **?** Is it a series of small steps or a giant leap forward?

Answering this question means discovering one of the determiners for the kind of framework you'll benefit most from.

Leadership Style

Your leadership team's style is another critical factor in choosing a framework. The leadership style espoused by your decision makers sets the tone for the rest of the organization.

> **?** Do leaders direct in a top-down approach or do they prefer collaborative approaches that empower employees to contribute their own ideas and expertise?

The framework you choose should complement your leadership style. For instance, an Agile change management framework may gel well with leaders focused on collaboration. Alternatively, Kotter's structure approach may be more suited for direct, top-down leadership.

Noting how your leaders generally approach decision making and employee engagement will help you identify a framework that enhances their strengths and addresses potential weaknesses.

Resource Availability

Finally, assess the resources available to your organization. These include time, budget, and expertise. Some frameworks require more investment in terms of time and resources than others.

For example, implementing Agile might require significant upfront training and coaching, while Kotter's model might be easier to implement with fewer resources. Be honest about your organization's capacity for change and choose a framework that is feasible and realistic given your constraints.

Remember ...

The goal is to choose a framework that not only aligns with your organization's current state but also *paves the way toward your envisioned future.* By meticulously assessing your organizational culture, size, type of change, leadership style, and resources, you're ensuring that your chosen framework is a strategic tool that guides your transformation journey toward your desired "North Star."

The most effective change management approach is one that is not only a good fit at the outset, but also adaptable and scalable to *accommodate the evolving needs of your organization.*

Quick Tips: Implementing Your Change Management Framework

Quick Tips

- *Secure Leadership Buy-In*: By making sure your top management and leadership are committed champions of the chosen framework, you pave the way for adoption across the rest of the organization.
- *Assemble Your Change Team*: The team should be equipped with the diverse skills required not only to execute tasks, but also to drive change across the rest of the organization.
- *Communicate the "Why"*: If your workforce understands the "why" behind your transformation and its benefits, they are more likely to contribute and buy into your plans.
- *Develop a Detailed Plan*: Transformation goals should be broken down into smaller, management chunks with clear timelines and responsibilities. In this way, you can track progress and identify roadblocks ahead of time.
- *Celebrate Quick Wins*: Build momentum and maintain motivations by recognizing and celebrating early successes. These

small victories are proof that change is possible, serving as motivation to spur on the rest of your plans.

- *Address Resistance Proactively*: Don't ignore or dismiss resistance. Instead, listen to concerns, address fears, and provide the support and resources employees need to adapt to the change.
- *Monitor Progress and Adapt*: Regularly assess your progress against goals and KPIs. Be prepared to adjust your plan based on feedback and results. Remember, change is iterative, and flexibility is key to success.
- *Embed the Change*: Don't just focus on short-term gains. Work to embed the new behaviors, processes, and systems into your organization's culture so that change becomes the new norm.

Your Framework, Your Guardrails

Selecting the right change management framework goes beyond following a prescribed path; it's about finding the guideposts that will keep your organization on track during your transformative journey. Consider the framework as a set of guardrails - providing you structure and support while allowing for flexibility and adaptation to your unique transformation journey.

By meticulously assessing your organizational culture, size, type of change, leadership style, and resources, you're ensuring that your chosen framework isn't just a theoretical concept, but a practical tool that enables you to confidently navigate the twists and turns of transformation, leading your team toward your desired "North Star."

Key Takeaways

- *Frameworks Provide Structure*: Change management frameworks serve as the backbone of your changes, giving structure to the complexities of your transformation. As a roadmap, they guide leaders through the process, aiding in risk anticipation and mitigation.

- *Multiple Frameworks Exist*: There are no one-size-fits-all approaches. Popular frameworks like Kotter's Eight-Step Process, the ADKAR Model, Lewin's Change Model, and Agile offer different perspectives and approaches to change management.
- *Choosing the Right Fit Is Crucial*: The right choice of framework for your organization will depend on several factors. These include company culture, size and complexity, type of change, leadership style, and the resources available.
- *Adaptability Is Key*: Frameworks should only serve as guidelines to your transformation, without limiting your adaptability. Be prepared to tailor your approach to specific contexts or needs, making sure it resonates with your team.
- *Prioritize Collaboration and Communication*: Regardless of the framework you choose, effective communication and collaboration are essential for transformation success. Ensure that all stakeholders understand the "why" behind the change and feel empowered to contribute.

CHAPTER 14

Technology and Data as Transformation Enablers

"Without big data analytics, companies are blind and deaf, wandering out onto the Web like deer on a freeway."

—**Geoffrey Moore**

Introduction: The Technological Landscape

It's not surprising that due to rapid advancements in the technological landscape during the past decades, technology and data have become not just tools for operational efficiency but strategic levers that can drive innovation, unlock new growth opportunities, and accelerate your transformation journey. Despite this:

> **?** Can your current systems handle the increased demands of a growing customer base?
> Can you make timely decisions based on updated real-time data?
> Are your employees equipped with the collaborative tools that allow them to work smarter, not harder?

Technology's Role in Transformations

While automation is often touted as a primary benefit of technology, its role in transformation goes much deeper. Technology can:

- *Empower Employees*: Imagine powerful CRM systems with data on clients' purchases, preferences, and past interactions, empowering your customer service representatives for personalized services, quicker issue resolution, and stronger client relationships.

- *Streamline Processes*: Apart from automating repetitive tasks, technology can optimize workflows and free up employees to work on higher-value activities. They will instead work on building customers relationships, brainstorming, or uncovering insights from data.

- *Enable Data-Driven Decision Making*: Real-time insights have become essential for informed and timely decision making. Collecting, analyzing, and interpreting data to identify trends, anticipate needs, and measure impacts can all be streamlined through technology.

- *Break Down Silos*: Cloud-based collaboration tools and communication platforms can connect employees across departments and locations, serving as an essential antidote for breaking down silos and driving innovation.

- *Enhance the Customer Experience*: From personalized product recommendations to self-service portals, technology can drastically improve how customers interact with your organization, leading to increased satisfaction and loyalty.

Quick Tips: Key Considerations for Technology Adoption

Quick
Tips

- *Alignment with Your Vision*: Introducing the latest gadgets will be useless if they do not align with your "North Star" vision and strategic goals. Make sure to assess utility before costly investments.
- *Change Management is Key*: New technologies are only as effective as they are widely adopted. Invest in employee training and support to create a tech-enabled culture within your organization.
- *Data Security and Privacy*: Increased reliance on technology means parallel investments in data security and privacy. Prioritize robust protocols and protections that protect sensitive information and ensure regulatory compliance.

Data Analytics as a Driver of Change

Think about the last time you made a major decision - perhaps purchasing a new car or planning a dream vacation.

> **?** Did you rely solely on gut instinct? Or did you research online, compare options, and analyze reviews?

Most likely, you used data to inform your choice.

In the same way, an organization's decisions must be based on a sound analysis of the vast amounts of data they generate - a game changer for any transformation.

Understanding Data-Driven Decision Making

Data analytics means extracting actionable insights from raw information. This could include identifying trends and patterns hidden in the sea of data collected. Correctly utilized, these insights guide all kinds of decision-making avenues, whether product development, marketing, or customer service. When every decision is strategically based on data, your likelihood of success increases.

By thoroughly understanding past trends, data analytics can also help predicting your organization's future. Models and forecasts of future operating environments or client response based on historical data can help you anticipate market shifts to adapt proactively.

The same models can also be used to identify bottlenecks and inefficiencies within your organization. Based on the data gathered, processes can then be optimized, reducing costs, enhancing services, and aligning your transformation to your strategic goals.

Quick Tips

Quick Tips: Implementing a Data-Driven Culture

- *Leadership Endorsement*: Organization-wide adoption of data-driven decisions means thorough adoption of the practice by its leaders. By prioritizing data when making decisions, leaders can inspire the change among the rest of their personnel.

- *Investment in Technology and Talent*: New technologies such as data management systems or analytical tools require your organization's investment. Concurrently and equally important is investing in skilled people who can translate the data into useful insights.
- *Continuous Learning and Adaptation*: A data-driven organization must also prioritize learning and flexibility. Analytical and data science innovations thrives in spaces with ongoing education and adaptation mindsets.

Ethical Considerations in Data Use

Collecting, storing, and utilizing large amounts of data inevitably requires the prioritization of privacy and its security.

Customers and employees must know and easily understand how your organization is using data about them. Apart from strictly complying to data protection regulations, your organization must always use data fairly and in a non-discriminatory way.

Safeguarding Your Transformation's (Data) Foundation

While technology and data analytics hold immense promise for your transformation, they also come with potential pitfalls.

> **?** How can you recognize when collected data is inaccurate and incomplete? How does it affect your analyses?
> What happens if sensitive client data is misplaced, lost, or stolen due to lax security?

Customers and employees agree to or allow for the collection of their data because they trust your organization will handle it correctly. Any security breaches, misuse, or lack of transparency may easily break that trust.

Data Quality	Data-driven decision making is built on sound analysis of accurate, complete, and consistent data. Flaws or discrepancies in your data can quickly throw you off track, leading to misguided decisions and ineffective strategies. Establish clear standards for how data is collected, stored, validated, maintained, cleaned, and regularly updated.
Data Governance	Clear policies and rulesets that define who has access to or is responsible for different sets of data must be clearly defined. These should comply with relevant regulations and create accountability and transparency, which builds trust with employees and customers.
Data Security	Investing in robust safety and security measures should be a given whenever storing or using large sets of data given the increasingly common and sophisticated cyberattacks. This typically involves encryption, access controls, and vulnerability assessments, serving as moats and fortified walls to your castle's valuable assets.

Remember that, particularly in transformations, data should be more than just interpreting a random set of numbers. Instead, you should make sure that the interpretation of the data and subsequently the actions you need to take during your transformation journey are based on effective data insights that can be gained through high standards for data quality, governance, and security.

Quick Tips

Quick Tips: Integrating Data Quality, Governance, and Security

- *Unified Data Management Framework*: Build a dedicated team of experts and representatives from across your organization to collaboratively create and enforce data policies that prioritize quality, governance, and security for your data.
- *Tools and Technologies for Data Integrity*: Implement a combination of data quality tools for cleaning and validating data, alongside security technologies like encryption and intrusion detection systems to safeguard data integrity.
- *Education and Cultural Change*: Develop regular training programs and promote a culture of data stewardship, ensuring all employees understand their role in maintaining data integrity and security.

- *Monitoring and Compliance*: Utilize continuous monitoring systems to oversee data usage and access, complemented by regular audits to assess the effectiveness of governance and security measures.
- *Privacy and Protection Techniques*: Enhance data protection through techniques like data anonymization and pseudonymization, and establish robust incident response protocols to address data breaches promptly.
- *Policy Review and Adaptation*: Regularly update and adapt data management policies to align with evolving technology and regulatory requirements, ensuring policies remain relevant and effective in new data usage contexts.

Leveraging Technology and Data Synergies

We've discussed the importance and power of aligning your technology infrastructure with your transformation goals and embracing data-driven decision making. Now, imagine the possibilities when these two elements work together in synergy, amplifying each other's impact and accelerating your journey.

A successful transformation requires an effective symbiosis of both technology tools and data. The right tech will empower your organization to collect and understand the data needed for informed decision making. On the other hand, the data, in turn, dictates the kind of technologies needed and how to implement them.

What results is a continuously improving cycle - a snowball effect for better data collection, more refined strategies, and further tech enhancements.

As you consider new technologies for your transformation, it's easy to get caught up in the excitement of cutting-edge solutions. But remember, not every new tool is the right fit for your organization; therefore, you need to take a moment to reflect on the following:

What are the specific data insights that will truly drive your transformation forward?
What are the most pressing questions you need answers to?

> Does the technology you're considering align with those needs, or is it more about keeping up with the competition?
>
> Will the technology seamlessly integrate with your existing systems, or will it create more complexity and data silos?
>
> Does it offer the robust security and governance features necessary to protect your valuable data assets?
>
> Most importantly, will it empower your team to make data-driven decisions at all levels of the organization, fostering a culture of continuous improvement?

Once you've chosen the right technology for your context, you'll be on the right track to fully utilize the potential of your collected data.

For example, a customer relationship management (CRM) system that is enabled by AI can go further than simple data collection from transactions, web interactions, or social media. Through machine learning it can additionally perform analyses on customer behavior, preferences, and financial goals.

With these insights, an organization can then customize services to target individual needs, take advantage of cross-selling opportunities, and improve risk management. It will therefore further drive across-the-board improvements that will ultimately deliver a better experience to customers.

Keep in mind that your data holds a wealth of valuable insights that can drive your transformation forward. As we've covered, it is then the right tech choices that will ultimately quicken data collection, break down data silos, and provide the real-time insights that empower your team.

Conclusion: The Strategic Power of Tech and Data

As we've seen in this chapter, technology and data are not just tools but strategic enablers that can revolutionize how your organization operates, serves customers, and ultimately achieves its transformation goals. By thoughtfully assessing your technological needs, carefully selecting the right solutions, and prioritizing data quality, governance, and security, you build a solid foundation for success.

Remember to employ tech that collects data and allows for its sound analysis in a way that they complement each other to accelerate your transformation and slingshot your organization toward your "North Star" vision.

Key Takeaways

- *Strategic Alignment*: Recognize the importance of tech and data beyond their value as mere tools. Utilize them as the strategic force multipliers that they are, aligning your investments with overarching goals and vision.
- *Data-Driven Decision Making*: Your organization must champion data-driven decision making by investing in the appropriate tools and empowering employees with the training and knowledge to properly make use of them.
- *Data Quality and Governance*: Your decisions can only be as good as the quality and reliability of the data behind them. Make sure this is well governed for responsible, ethical, and secure use.
- *Technology as an Enabler*: Invest in tech that goes beyond simple data collection. Instead, these tools should empower your team to deliver the best enhanced customer experience possible through better access and understanding of data and process automation
- *Synergy of Technology and Data*: The most impactful transformations leverage the synergy between technology and data. Technology enables better data collection and analysis, while data insights inform better technology choices and implementation strategies.
- *The Human Element*: While technology is a powerful enabler, its success hinges on human adoption. Invest in change management, training, and support to ensure employees embrace new tools and processes.
- *Continuous Evolution*: Technology and data are constantly evolving. Continuously evaluate your systems and processes to ensure they remain aligned with your goals and capable of supporting your transformation journey.

CHAPTER 15

Keeping Your Transformation on Track

"To improve is to change; to be perfect is to change often."
—Winston Churchill

Introduction: The Transformation Landscape

Let's go back to our metaphor comparing your organization's transformation to a cross-country road trip. We've covered the preparations: a map, a fully checked car, along with enthusiastic and helpful passengers.

But even with the most meticulous planning, would you simply set your coordinates and set off without expecting any hitches? No - you'd keep an eye on your fuel gauge, double check your maps for alternate routes and adjust your driving depending on the roads encountered.

Similarly, transformation efforts require ongoing attention and adaptability. So far, we've laid the foundation, harmonized our efforts across the organization, integrated key processes, and fostered a culture of innovation. Now, the journey continues.

How can we make sure our efforts are sustained and that the organization grows in alignment with our long-term vision for it?

Such assurances are obtained through a disciplined approach, careful portfolio management and a robust system for measuring progress. Additionally, it requires the flexibility to adjust strategies as unexpected obstacles are encountered while being ready to make the most of any opportunities.

Project and Portfolio Management in Transformation

Think about the ways you usually manage complex projects and initiatives.

> **?** Are risks clearly identified, monitored, tracked, and addressed
> through necessary adjustments?
> Do you confidently allocate resources to support all moving parts
> toward a common goal?

Transformations highlight the importance of these considerations, raising the stakes alongside complexity and the need for coordination. This is where portfolio, program, and project management (PPM) strategies shine.

These strategies provide the structure and guidance that allows you to:

Maintain Strategic Alignment

Projects should be chosen based on how closely they support your transformational goals, with resources allocated for maximum impact. These should in turn be measured with metrics that best reflect their effectiveness, ensuring clear targets and proper prioritization.

Achieve Portfolio Oversight

Live dashboards allow for pertinent insights into a project's current status by measuring resources utilization and progress. Proactively tackle potential risks by pre-planning and addressing them early in a project's life cycle, making necessary adjustments to the project's portfolio based on the latest reviews, reporting, and data.

Build Governance Structures

Establish oversight and accountability throughout the transformation process. This involves setting up governance committees tasked with making pivotal decisions regarding project continuation, resource distribution, and strategic alignment. Regular review cycles will allow you to monitor set objective to maintain adherence to the project while robust communication keeps stakeholders properly informed.

Leverage Technology

Project management software allows for progress and resources tracking while collaboration tools facilitate communication among project members, utilizing data analytics software to extract actionable insights. These technologies serve as essential tools for decision making and efficiency across the portfolio.

Quick Tips: Implementing Effective Project and Portfolio Management

- *Start with Your "North Star"*: Project Portfolio Management (PPM) strategies should always point toward your North Star, ensuring that every initiative serves as stepping stones toward its achievement.

- *Establish a Clear Governance Structure*: Project prioritization and resource allocation decisions should be made by dedicated governance committees that include stakeholders from across the organization, ensuring diverse perspectives and preventing bottlenecks.
- *Define Roles and Responsibilities*: Outline clear roles and responsibilities for project managers, program managers, and portfolio managers. When responsibilities are clearly defined, accountability is heightened and confusion avoided.
- *Develop a Comprehensive Project Portfolio*: Categorize all your transformation initiatives by type, priority, and impact to create a holistic view of the entire journey.
- *Implement a Robust Risk Management Process*: Identify potential risks to your projects, assess their impact, and develop mitigation strategies. This might involve creating contingency plans, reallocating resources, or adjusting project timelines as needed.
- *Leverage Technology*: Project management software can help track progress, manage resources, and facilitate collaboration. Insights and improvements can be gained and identified through data analytics tools.
- *Foster a Culture of Continuous Improvement*: Your approach, including the holistic project portfolio should be regularly reviewed and optimized. Your team and stakeholders' feedback helps identify lessons learned and apply insights.

Transformation-Focused Project Management

The complexity inherent to transformations requires work that goes beyond traditional project management principles. Multiple stakeholders, interconnected systems, and high uncertainty mean that fixed plans and rigid timelines can no longer apply.

Additionally, transformation initiatives often demand significant changes in behavior, mindset, and culture that are not typically addressed in the traditional project management practices. Lastly, the business landscape is not static and constantly presents new challenges and opportunities.

All of these realities necessitate project management strategies and practices that are more adaptable and flexible, strategies that can roll with the unpredictable punches each transformation throws. A solution could be incorporating agile methodologies into your project management approach to prioritize flexibility, collaboration, and continuous improvement.

At the end of the day, keep in mind that you need to create a structure that not only supports your transformation goals but also adapts to the inevitable twists and turns of the journey ahead.

Risk Management: Not Your Enemy But Your Ally

Risk management may conjure unpleasant images of mountains of paperwork and endless meetings. More often though, the reality is that effective risk management during your transformation means minimizing costly setbacks as you take bold steps toward your vision.

Countless resources cover the intricacies of identifying, assessing, and mitigating risk. Here, we'll highlight risk management in the context of its importance for your transformation.

The emergence of risks during your transformation journey is a reality, and to be successful you need to move past perceiving risk management as an odious, overly bureaucratic process to get over with. Instead, keep in mind that when properly integrated, the process enhances your agility and ensures your transformation can swiftly adapt to changes by:

- *Proactively addressing potential pitfalls* that could impact timelines or outcomes.
- *Ensuring resources are used efficiently*, minimizing waste on unexpected issues.
- *Enhancing decision making* with a clear understanding of potential risks and their impacts.

Risks can arise across various areas during your transformation, from people and processes to technology and external factors. Your job is to understand, prioritize, and mitigate those risks that could have the most significant impact on your transformation journey.

Keep in mind that risk management cannot exist as a one-and-done checklist within your organization. Instead, an iterative and proactive approach is what truly empowers teams to embrace changes confidently, safe in the knowledge that they are prepared for challenges.

Managing Expectations: A Critical Tool for Staying on Track

How can a project ever be successfully completed without a common vision for what success looks like?

Can change be achieved if your on-the-ground team struggles to achieve small wins due to short deadlines while concurrently the CEO dreams of overnight market disruptions and customers expect an overhauled experience?

This all-too-common scenario highlights a silent threat to your transformation's success: *misaligned expectations.*

This breeding ground for frustration, distrust, and dwindling support can create a domino effect of negative consequences. Teams may feel pressured, leading to rushed decisions and burnout. Faced with unrealistic expectations, leaders might resort to micromanagement or even blame tactics, while customers, disappointed by undelivered promises, lose trust and loyalty.

This is why managing expectations should not be an afterthought, but rather a critical consideration for staying on track. This means a shared understanding of the transformation journey among all stakeholders, including its challenges, opportunities, and potential setbacks.

However, effective expectation management should extend beyond merely averting disappointment. Instead, engage stakeholders to build trust, collaboration, and collective commitment. By ensuring that everyone is invested in the journey, you can maintain support and keep the transformation on track.

Quick Tips: Strategies for Setting Realistic Expectations

Quick
Tips

- *Transparency Is Key*: Your transformation's complexities and potential roadblocks should be communicated upfront,

demonstrating an understanding of the realities behind implementing your ideas rather than an over-eagerness to leap
forward to the implementation. This will build trust in what
you want to achieve.

- *Communicate Early and Often*: Regular and consistent updates
on progress, encountered issues, and reached milestones ensure
that your team and stakeholders are not left in the dark and
maintains tack with opportunities for feedback.

- *Engage Stakeholders*: By involving stakeholders in your planning, expectations are aligned ahead of time, fostering a sense
of collective ownership for the transformation.

- *Focus on Tangible Outcomes*: Highlight your transformation's
pragmatic improvements instead of making vague promises
about its potential, giving stakeholders concrete targets to look
forward to and evaluate progress against.

Monitoring Progress and Making Strategic Adjustments

Take a moment to reflect on your transformation journey so far.

> **?** Can you confidently explain what success for your transforma-
> tion looks like? Is progress measured diligently to ensure efforts
> align with that vision?

The answers to these questions are critical for ensuring your transformation stays on course.

Dynamic Application of Established KPIs

Remember those key performance indicators (KPIs) we discussed in
Chapter 4? These metrics are the gauges on your transformation dashboard, providing real-time insights into your progress and allowing you
to make informed decisions.

However, KPIs aren't static measures. As your transformation evolves,
so too must your metrics. Make sure to continuously reevaluate whether

these metrics are still relevant, align with your changing priorities and reflect your initiatives' desired impacts.

For example, at the start of your transformation you might be seeking to improve your employees' engagement, and have therefore centered your KPIs around participation rates. Once your transformation journey progresses, you may instead focus on measuring the productivity, innovation, and customer satisfaction.

Integrating Feedback Mechanisms

Remember, data isn't the only compass you have at your disposal. Qualitative feedback from stakeholders can color in the sterile lines that data draws, offering invaluable insights into what works, what doesn't, and why.

This means surveys, focus groups, and open forums to better understand your transformation's effectiveness and find out how to improve it. Seek feedback at all stages of your journey to make sure all voices are considered when making decisions.

Strategic Adjustments

Based on your data and feedback, be prepared to shift resources, alter project scopes, or even redefine timelines. These adjustments should be made strategically, always with the goal of aligning your efforts with the overarching objectives of your organization.

Remember, transformation is rarely a linear path. In the same way, your approach to measurement and strategies should adapt to its twists and turns, making sure you stay on track and thrive in the face of adversities.

Securing Success in Your Transformation Journey

We've covered how robust project and portfolio management practices together with proactive risk and expectation management can help your organization to respond to immediate challenges and lay the groundwork for sustained success.

With this in mind, the true measure of success will be your organization's adaptability and growth throughout the transformation's progress, a shift from the traditional mindset that equates success to reaching pre-defined targets.

The formula, although challenging, is, therefore, clear. You need to look at your transformation journey with a strategic, adaptable mindset with a clear focus on your long-term vision.

Key Takeaways

- *Transformation Requires Active Management*: Successfully staying on course throughout your transformation journey means continuously monitoring, adapting, and course-correcting as needed.
- *Project and Portfolio Management (PPM)*: PPM serves as a backbone for your complex changes by making sure resources are well allocated, risks are proactively managed, and progress is tracked consistently.
- *Measuring Progress with KPIs*: Measure the success of your transformation using key performance indicators (KPIs). These essential tools should adapt alongside your initiatives and integrate into your daily operations.
- *Stakeholder Feedback Is Crucial*: By collecting feedback from as wide a variety of employees, customers, and stakeholders as possible, you can identify areas for improvement and strategy adjustment.
- *Strategic Adjustments Are Key to Success*: Be prepared to adapt your plans based on feedback, changing market conditions, and emerging risks. Flexibility is essential for staying on course and achieving your long-term vision.
- *Risk Management is Essential*: As the name implies, risk assessment is crucial for proactively identifying potential obstacles. Utilize insights from this assessment to mitigate impacts and adapt your transformation as needed.
- *Managing Expectations is Crucial*: Align stakeholder expectations with the reality of the transformation journey. Be transparent about challenges and focus on communicating tangible outcomes to maintain support and engagement.

Case Study: FINxP PAYMENTS - A FINTECH TRANSFORMATION JOURNEY (Continued)

(The company's name has been changed to protect its identity.)

With numerous projects underway and change happening rapidly, we recognized the importance of maintaining a steady course toward our "North Star." Our transformation involved many moving parts, and we knew that avoiding overwhelm and burnout was crucial. To achieve this, we needed to ensure our efforts were controlled, yet dynamic, fostering agility while also driving innovation.

Choosing the Right Change Management Frameworks

We carefully selected a change management framework that aligned with our company culture, size, and our "North Star" vision. From the various methodologies available, careful consideration led us to Kotter's Eight-Step Process and Agile methodologies. We adopted the hybrid approach to provide a structured roadmap while allowing us the flexibility to adapt and respond to challenges as they arose.

Technology and Data as Transformation Enablers

Technology was the backbone of our transformation. By striking up partnerships with cloud providers, we upgraded legacy systems with the scalability, agility, and security required to handle the growing number of transactions we processed. We also invested in advanced data analytics platforms and AI-powered tools to streamline compliance, detect fraud, and gain valuable insights into customer behavior.

Of course, we recognized that it wasn't just about shiny new tech. By prioritizing the quality of data we collected, we made sure our new systems had the accurate, reliable, and well-governed input required to harness their potential.

A change in the organization's culture toward more data-driven approaches was invaluable. For example, we were initially pursuing a product idea that, after releasing a minimum viable product (MVP), received un-enthusiastic customer feedback. Data insights allowed us to quickly pivot to an alternative that resonated better with our target audience.

Keeping the Transformation on Track

Tracking progress was the next important hurdle to tackle once the transformation was under way. Real-time dashboards for FINxP Payment's key performance indicators allowed us to gain insights into our progress. At the same time, these revealed areas that needed attention, giving us the data to confidently course-correct as needed.

The cross-functional change management team we put together to oversee the process played a pivotal role. They facilitated team communication, identified risks ahead of time, and made sure our changes kept us on track to achieve the "North Star" vision. Our success was owed to this quick-adapting collaborative approach.

Outcomes and Impact

Through these concentrated efforts, our transformation became a resounding success. The new mobile app we developed received rave reviews from our customers, who appreciated its intuitive interface and seamless payment experience. Transaction speeds increased dramatically, and our compliance processes became far more efficient and accurate, thanks to our AI-powered tools.

Perhaps most importantly, our employees embraced the change. The knowledge-sharing platform and personalized learning journeys we launched left them feeling empowered and excited to bring more innovative contributions to FINxP payments. The infectious enthusiasm spread throughout the organization, leading to a sense of purpose and pride.

As a result of our successful transformation, FINxP Payments not only weathered the storm of increased competition but also emerged as a leader in the fintech industry. Within two years, this led to a doubling of our revenue alongside a reputation for reliability, innovation, and customer-centricity.

The SHIFT framework provided us with a clear roadmap and the tools we needed to turn our vision into reality. By embracing change as a constant, fostering a culture of innovation, and empowering our employees, we were able to transform our organization and achieve lasting success in the ever-evolving fintech landscape.

Explore Further

Ancillary questions and supporting materials related to this case study are available to help you apply the concepts introduced in this stage. These resources can be accessed through the QR code provided in the Preface section.

Conclusion

Reflection on the Journey

In winding up our exploration of the SHIFT framework for transformations, let's reflect on the journey we've made and take stock of what lies ahead. In this book, we've taken a look at the many different and complex factors that go into planning and executing a successful transformation. That means the fundamental principles, strategies, and tools that empower leaders to embrace change as a catalyst for their organizations' growth and innovation.

The SHIFT framework - Start, Harmonize, Integrate, Facilitate, and Transform - has served as our guide, providing a structured yet adaptable approach to tackling the multifaceted challenges that arise during any transformation.

Whether defining a clear vision or building an adaptable workforce, fostering innovation or implementing change effectively, the SHIFT model empowers you with way to build stronger, more agile, and customer-centric organizations.

Looking Ahead: The Ever-Changing Landscape

The world is in constant flux, and the landscape of organizational transformation is no exception.

Emerging technologies such as artificial intelligence, blockchain, and advanced analytics are reshaping business processes and customer interactions. Apart from new technologies, more flexible work models such as remote or hybrid working also present new challenges and opportunities for organizations. Customers are also becoming more digitally and tech-savvy, with expectations for personalized and seamless, digitally enabled experiences rising.

To navigate these changes and remain competitive, organizations must embrace a future-ready mindset. This means prioritizing agility, being data-driven in decision making, and maintaining a focus on the customer experience. The principles you've learned in this book will equip you to not just weather these changes, but to leverage them for growth and innovation.

Final Thoughts and Reflections

Remember, transformation is not a one-time event, but a continuous journey. It therefore requires a strategic mindset, a commitment to continuous learning, and the courage to challenge the status quo.

It also means embracing this journey with an open mind and a clear vision, considering every challenge as an opportunity to learn and grow. Finally, it means, shaping a future where your organizational culture becomes your biggest asset toward overcoming all sorts of challenges.

To reach this goal, be sure to take a moment to reflect on your own transformation experiences:

> **?** What challenges have you faced, and how did you overcome them?
>
> What successes have you celebrated, and what can you learn from them?
>
> How can you apply these lessons to future initiatives?

Your Transformation Starts Today

The time for action is here. There is no "perfect" moment to start your transformation journey - it only requires a bold first step.

Invest firstly in yourself. A personal growth plan with opportunities to explore new technologies and methodologies can supercharge your transformation. For a broader and more informed perspective, connect with peers and industry leaders to tap into the collective knowledge of your professional networks.

Most importantly, inspire your team by becoming the change leaders your organization needs. Your end goal should be a vibrant culture filled with continuous improvement and innovation - one that includes voices and ideas from across your organization, where everyone is empowered to contribute their unique share.

Forget about just surviving. Transformations are moments to thrive and excel in. Your team's shared commitment to growth and adaptability means not only weathering the storms of change but coming out the other side stronger and more knowledgeable.

The power to transform lies within you and your team!

Embrace the journey, stay true to your vision, and, with your team, create a lasting legacy of innovation and growth that will benefit your organization for years to come.

About the Author

Jonathan Spiteri is the founder and CEO of Strategy and Transformation Services Ltd, and a recognized expert in strategic change and enterprise transformation. He has led complex, cross-industry programs focused on organizational transformation, digital innovation, and enterprise governance. His work with multinational organizations including the UK, France, Australia, Nigeria, India, Ukraine, Romania, and Malta has delivered measurable results in strategic planning, innovation, operational efficiency, and leadership alignment.

His expertise spans the entire life cycle of strategic change: from vision-setting and business case development to implementation, governance, and benefits realization. He has established and led Strategy, Transformation, Professional Services, Project Management Offices (PMOs), Information Technology (IT), and Digital Offices, each acting as a catalyst for agility, innovation, and sustainable growth.

In addition to his delivery work, Jonathan contributes to the broader professional community through keynote speaking, training, and coaching. His dedication to development and thought leadership is reflected in his work with the Project Management Institute (PMI) Malta Chapter, where he played a pivotal role in its creation and strategic positioning. Through his leadership, the chapter has become a central hub for project, change and leadership management excellence and community engagement.

A strong advocate for continuous learning, Jonathan holds the Axelos ProPath Portfolio Director certification, with practitioner-level credentials in MoP®, P3O®, MSP®, PRINCE2 Agile®, and MoR®. He is also a certified SAFe® 6 Practice Consultant (SPC), Project Management Professional (PMP), and Six Sigma Black Belt. He holds an MBA from the University of Malta and a diploma in computing and information systems from the University of London.

Index